Python Programming
for Students and Beginners

Python Programming for Students and Beginners

Coding stories for high school students, kids, and new programmers

by Ashutosh Shashi

Python programming for Students and Beginners: Coding stories for high school students, kids, and new programmers

DEDICATION

To all the curious minds—young and old—who are not afraid to ask questions, experiment, and explore the world of coding.
May this book inspire your journey into the magical world of Python!

Table of Contents

Introduction

Welcome to "**Python programming for Students and Beginners:
Coding stories for high school students, kids, and new
programmers**"
This book is your gateway to the world of coding. Whether you are 8 or 80
or anywhere in between, Python is the perfect place to start your journey
into programming. Python is one of the most popular programming
languages in the world—and the best part? It is fun and easy to learn!
You do not need to be a computer expert or a math wizard to get started.
All you need is curiosity, a little bit of patience, and a computer! In this
book, you will learn how to write code in Python from scratch, and by the
end, you will be building your own simple programs and games.

What is Python?

Python is a programming language—a way for humans to talk to
computers. Just like we use different languages to communicate with each
other, we use Python to give computer instructions. It is like giving your
computer a list of steps to follow. Python is used to build all kinds of
things: websites, games, apps, and even robots!

Why Python?

Python is perfect for beginners because it is simple to read and write. In
fact, Python looks a lot like normal English! But do not let that fool you—
Python is also incredibly powerful. Big companies like Google, YouTube,
and NASA use Python every day to do amazing things.

What Will You Learn?

This book will start with the basics—how to install Python on your
computer and write your first program. Do not worry if you have never
written code before. I will guide you through every step with fun examples,
stories, and projects that make learning Python a blast.

How This Book Works

Each chapter in this book is like a mini-adventure. You will learn something new, try out some code, and have time to experiment with what you have learned. You will start small, writing simple programs, but by the end, you will build games, create interactive programs, and even write your code from scratch!

And do not worry—I will be right here to guide you every step of the way. So, grab your computer, open this book, and get ready for an exciting journey into the world of Python!

Chapter 1: Getting Ready to Code

What You Will Need: A Computer, Python, and an Internet Connection

A Computer

You will need a computer to write and run your Python programs. It doesn't matter if it is a Windows PC, a Mac, or a Linux machine—Python works on all of them! Here is a quick guide to the type of computer that will work:

- Windows: Any computer running Windows 7, 8, 10, or 11 will do just fine.
- Mac: Python will work on any macOS version if you use a Mac.
- Linux: If you are running Ubuntu, Debian, or any other Linux distribution, you are good to go!

Python does not require high computer specifications. Writing Python code on an old or basic computer is perfectly acceptable.

Python

Python is the primary tool we will use to write and run code. Don't worry if you don't have it installed yet—we will walk through how to install Python in just a minute. Python is completely free to download and use.

An Internet Connection

You will need the internet to download Python and some other helpful tools. Once everything is set up, you won't require the internet to write code, but for now, you should ensure that you can download the software you need.

What's Next?

Now that we know what we need, it is time to set everything up. In the next part of this chapter, we will walk through the process of installing Python on your computer, whether you are using Windows, Mac, or Linux.

Let's get started!

Setting up Python on your computer (Windows, Mac, Linux).

Now that you know what you will need, let's move on to setting up Python on your computer. Whether you are using Windows, Mac, or Linux, don't worry! We will walk through each step carefully. Follow along, and soon, you will be ready to code!

Step 1: Downloading Python

We need to download Python before we can install it. Here is how:

Visit the Python Website
- Open your web browser (like Chrome, Firefox, or Edge).
- Type in python.org and press Enter.
- You'll see a yellow button that says Download Python 3.x.x (The version number may change). Click this button.

> Fun Fact!
> Did you know Python updates regularly? The version number keeps changing as Python gets better and better!

Step 2: Installing Python

Now that you have downloaded Python, let's install it on your computer.
2.1. Installing Python on Windows.
Open the Installer:

After the download finishes, locate the file you downloaded. It will be called something like python-3.x.x.exe. Double-click the file to open it.

Important Step!

Before clicking anything, check the "Add Python to PATH" box. This is very important because it ensures your computer knows where to find Python.

Install Python:

Click Install Now. The installer will begin copying files and setting everything up for you. This may take a few minutes, so sit tight!

Finish the Installation:

When it is done, you will see a message that says Setup was successful. That's it! Python is now installed on your computer.

2.2. Installing Python on Mac

Open the Installer:

Find the file you downloaded (python-3.x.x-macosx.pkg). Double-click it to open.

Follow the Instructions:

The Python installer will guide you through the process. Just click **Continue** and follow the steps. You may be asked to enter your Mac password during the installation.

Complete the Installation:

When the installation finishes, Python will be ready to use on your Mac!

2.3. Installing Python on Linux

Verify if Python is already installed.

Most Linux systems come with Python pre-installed, but we will check to make sure.

Open your **Terminal** and type:

```
python3 –version
```

If you see a version number, you are good to go. If not, follow the steps below.

Installing Python Using Terminal:

If Python is not installed, type the following command into your Terminal:

```
sudo apt-get install python3
```

Press **Enter** and follow the instructions on the screen. You will install Python quickly.

Step 3: Verifying Your Python Installation

Once Python is installed, let's make sure it's working.
Verifying on Windows, Mac, and Linux
Open the Command Prompt or Terminal:
Check Python Version:
In the Command Prompt in Window, type:

```
python –version
```

In the terminal in Mac or Linux, type:
python3 --version

Press **Enter**. If everything is installed correctly, the displayed version number will be like Python 3.x.x. That means Python is ready to go!

```
ashutoshshashi@Ashutoshs-MacBook-Pro ~ % python3 --version
Python 3.12.5
ashutoshshashi@Ashutoshs-MacBook-Pro ~ %
```

Congratulations! 🎉 **You've installed Python!**

Now that you have set up Python, you are ready to write your first program. But before that, we need one more thing—a code editor to write your Python code. In the next section, we will install **Visual Studio Code (VS Code)**, a free and easy-to-use editor.

Installing a code editor (VS Code)

Now that you have installed Python, you will need a place to write your code. This is where a **code editor** comes in! Think of it as your Python notebook, where you will write all your coding adventures. One of the best (and free!) code editors out there is **Visual Studio Code (VS Code)**. Let's walk through the process of downloading, installing, and setting up VS Code, step by step.

Step 1: Downloading VS Code

1.1. Go to the VS Code Website

1. Open your web browser (Chrome, Firefox, Edge, etc.).
2. In the address bar, type code.visualstudio.com and press Enter.
3. You'll see a big blue button that says Download for Your OS (the website will detect your operating system—Windows, Mac, or Linux).
4. Click the blue Download button.

Fun Fact!
Did you know that VS Code is one of the most popular code editors in the world? Millions of programmers use it to write everything from games to websites!

Step 2: Installing VS Code

2.1. Installing VS Code on Windows

1. Once the file is downloaded, find it in your Downloads folder. It will be called something like VSCodeSetup-x.x.x.exe.
2. Double-click the file to open the installer.
3. A window will pop up. Check the box that says "Add to PATH." This will ensure that your computer knows where to find VS Code.
4. Click Next, then Install.
5. After a few moments, the installation will finish. Click Finish to open VS Code.

2.2. Installing VS Code on Mac

1. Once the download is finished, find the file called VSCode-darwin-x64.zip in your Downloads folder.
2. Double-click the file to unzip it.
3. You'll see the Visual Studio Code app. Drag it to your Applications folder.
4. Once it's in the Applications folder, double-click it to open VS Code.

2.3. Installing VS Code on Linux

1. For Linux users, open your Terminal.
2. Use the following command to install VS Code:

```
sudo apt update
sudo apt install code
```

3. Follow the on-screen instructions and VS Code will be installed.

> Fun Fact:
> Did you know that VS Code was originally created by Microsoft, but it is completely free to use? You don't need to pay a cent, even though it is packed with powerful features.

Step 3: Personalizing VS Code (Optional)

Now that you have VS Code installed and running Python code, you can personalize it!

Themes:
- You can change the look of VS Code by going to File > Preferences > Color Theme. Choose a dark theme or a light theme—whatever suits your style!

Fonts:
- If you want bigger or smaller text, go to File > Preferences > Settings. In the search bar, type Font Size, and you can adjust it to make your code easier to read.

> Fun Fact:
> VS Code lets you change how it looks with themes and fonts! You can make it look like a space station, a vintage computer, or even a typewriter!

Installing the Python Extension in VS Code

Now that you have got **Visual Studio Code (VS Code)** installed and ready to go, it's time to teach VS Code how to understand Python. This is where the **Python Extension** comes in. Think of it as giving your code editor superpowers, so it can help you write Python code, catch your mistakes, and make coding more fun and easier!

In this chapter, we will take things step-by-step. By the end, you will be able to write Python code in VS Code like a pro!

Step 1: Opening VS Code

Imagine VS Code as your magic coding notebook. Every time you want to write Python spells (code), you need to open it. Let's do that now!

1. Windows: Press the Windows Key, type Visual Studio Code, and click on it to open.
2. Mac: Open your Applications folder, find Visual Studio Code, and double-click it.
3. Linux: Open your terminal and type: Press Enter to open VS Code. code

Once VS Code opens, you will see a welcome screen with many helpful options. But we are here to add Python to our coding notebook, so let's move on!

Fun Fact:
VS Code is like a superhero for coders! It's completely free, but it's packed with powers to help programmers write all kinds of code—games, websites, apps, and more!

Step 2: Finding the Extensions Panel

We need to install the **Python Extension** to give VS Code its superpowers. The extension is like a special tool that helps you write Python code.

On the left-hand side of VS Code, you will see a vertical toolbar with icons. These icons are like shortcuts to different parts of VS Code. Let's find the one we need:

1. Look for the icon that looks like four squares. This is the Extensions icon. It is like a toolbox where you can find all kinds of tools (extensions) to make VS Code more powerful.

2. Click on the Extensions icon, and a new panel will open up on the left. This is the Extensions Marketplace, where we can find the Python Extension!

Step 3: Searching for the Python Extension

Now, let's find the Python Extension. It is like looking for the right tool in a big toolbox.
1. At the top of the Extensions panel, you will see a search bar.
2. In the search bar, type the word Python and press Enter.

You will see a list of extensions appear. The one we are looking for should be right at the top. It's called **Python** and it is created by **Microsoft**.

Fun Fact:
The Python Extension for VS Code has been downloaded more than 30 million times! That's more than the population of Australia. Imagine that—millions of coders around the world using the same tool as you!

Step 4: Installing the Python Extension

Here is where the magic happens. Once we install the Python Extension, VS Code will understand how to work with Python code. It is like teaching your coding notebook how to read Python!
1. Next to the Python extension by Microsoft, you will see a blue "Install" button. Click on it.
2. Once you click it, VS Code will automatically download and install the Python Extension for you. This should only take a few seconds.
3. After the extension is installed, the blue "Install" button will change to a green "Uninstall" button. Don't click the green button! This means the extension has been successfully installed, and you are ready.

Step 5: Activating Python in VS Code

The Python Extension is installed, but there's one more thing we need to do—activate it! Once activated, VS Code will start helping you write Python code.

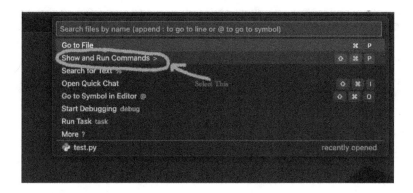

And then

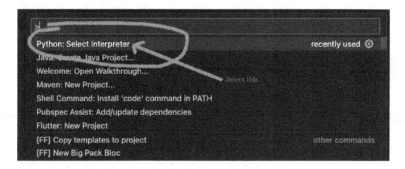

And Then

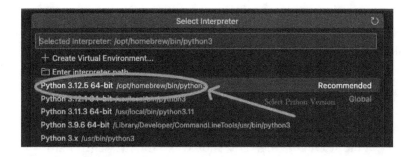

1. In the VS Code's top menu, click View, then select Command Palette from the dropdown. You can also press Ctrl + Shift + P (Windows/Linux) or Cmd + Shift + P (Mac) to open the Command Palette quickly.
2. In the Command Palette, type:

Python: Select Interpreter

and press Enter.

3. A list of Python versions installed on your computer will appear. Select the version you installed earlier (you can check the version using python --version in your terminal or command prompt).

4. Once you select the interpreter, VS Code will start recognizing Python code. This means it can now help you run and debug your Python programs!

Step 6: Testing the Python Extension

Now that everything is set up, let's write a quick Python program to ensure everything works.

1. In VS Code, click on File at the top, then select New File. A blank file will appear.

2. At the top, click File > Save As and save the file as test.py. Make sure it ends with .py, which tells VS Code it is a Python file.

3. In the blank file, type the following Python code:

```
print("I am learning Python!")
```

4. Now, let's run the code. Click on Run at the top of VS Code, then select Run Without Debugging. You should see the message "I am learning Python!" at the bottom of the screen in the Terminal.

Fun Fact:
Running Python code is like telling a computer to do something amazing. Every time you write a program and run it, you're creating something brand new!

What's Next?

Now that you have installed and activated the Python Extension, your coding notebook (VS Code) has powered up completely and is ready to assist you in writing Python code. In the next chapter, we will dive deeper into writing your first few Python programs and learn some cool tricks along the way.

Chapter 2: Writing Your First Python Program

What is a program?

Imagine you are the commander of a spaceship, and your mission is to explore new planets. But you can not pilot the spaceship on your own—you need a team of robots to help you. You have to tell the robots what to do step by step, like:

1. Step 1: Start the engines.
2. Step 2: Set the coordinates for the next planet.
3. Step 3: Begin the countdown.
4. Step 4: Blast off!

If the robots follow your instructions strictly, the spaceship will take off and head to the right planet. If they make a mistake or skip a step, the spaceship could end up lost in space!

A **program** works just like this. It is a list of instructions that the computer follows, step by step, to complete a task. The task could be something simple, like showing your name on the screen, or something complicated, like running a video game or controlling a robot.

Exploring Examples of Programs

Let's break this down into real-world examples that show how programs work, so you can see how powerful they are.

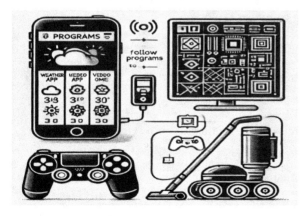

Example 1: The Weather App on Your Phone

You open your phone's weather app, which shows the current temperature, tells you if it is sunny or rainy, and even shows a forecast for the next few days. Behind the scenes, there is a program running that follows these steps:

1. Check your location.
2. Connect to a weather service to get the latest weather data.
3. Display the current weather on your phone.
4. Update the forecast every few minutes.

This is a **program**! It follows a list of instructions to ensure that you always know whether you need an umbrella.

Example 2: Making a Sandwich (A Real-Life Program!)

You might not realize it, but you follow programs every day without even thinking about it. Let's look at the steps involved in making a sandwich:

1. Get two slices of bread.
2. Spread butter on one slice.
3. Spread jelly on the other slice.
4. Put the two slices together.

This is a **program**! You are following a step-by-step process to make the sandwich. If you skip a step or do things out of order, you might end up with jelly all over your hands!

Example 3: A Simple Program in Python

Now, let's translate this idea into a simple Python program. Imagine you want the computer to show the phrase **"I love pizza!"** on the screen. You will write a simple program to make it happen.
Here's the code:

```
print("I love pizza!")
```

In this code:
- The print() command tells the computer to show the text inside the parentheses.
- The text "I love pizza!" is the message that the computer will display.

When the computer follows this program, it will show exactly what you told it to, just like following the steps to make a sandwich or check the weather.

Why Programs Are Like Recipes

Think of a program like a recipe. Just like a recipe tells you how to make cookies, a program tells the computer how to do something. Each step is important, and it must be followed in the right order. If you skip a step in a recipe, the cookies might not turn out right. If you skip a step in a program, the computer might not know what to do!

Let's compare a recipe and a program:

- **Recipe Example**:
    1. Preheat the oven.
    2. Mix the ingredients.
    3. Bake the cookies.
    4. Let them cool.

- **Program Example (Python)**:
    1. Ask the user for their name.
    2. Say hello to the user by name.
    3. Thank the user for participating.

Here is what the Python program would look like:

```
name = input("What is your name? ")
print("Hello, " + name + "!")
print("Thank you for participating!")
```

In this program:
- input("What is your name? ") asks the user for their name.

- print("Hello, " + name + "!") says hello to the user, using their name.
- print("Thank you for participating!") thanks the user.

The Power of Programs

Programs give computers their power. Without programs, computers would be expensive boxes that sit there and do nothing! Everything you do on a computer, whether it's playing a game, browsing the internet, or even turning it on, is driven by programs.

Things You Can Do with Programs:
- Create Websites: Programs control how websites look, what buttons do, and how information is displayed.
- Build Video Games: Every character, movement, and interaction in a video game is driven by programs.
- Control Robots: Programs are used to control robots, from vacuum cleaners to space rovers!

Programs Everywhere: A World Full of Code

It is easy to think that programs only live inside computers, but that is false. Programs are everywhere! For example:
- Your Smart TV: There is a program behind the scenes that makes it change channels, turn the volume up and down, and show movies.
- Your Car: Newer cars use programs to monitor speed, help you park, and even control the brakes in an emergency.
- Video Games: Every game you play has a program running in the background that controls what happens when you press a button or move a joystick.

The Interpreter: Your Code's Translator

Now, you might wonder, "How does the computer understand my Python code?" After all, computers do not speak English, and they do not speak Python! That is where the **interpreter** comes in.

Imagine you are speaking English, but the computer only understands a language called **binary**, which is made up of 0s and 1s. The interpreter's job is translating your Python code into binary, so the computer knows what to do. The interpreter reads your code line by line, turning it into instructions the computer can follow.

Writing and Running Your First Python Program

Now that you know what a program is, it's time to write your first one! You don't need to be an expert to get started—in fact, this is the fun part where you get to tell the computer what to do. We will write a simple program that tells the computer to greet us with a message. This program is famous in the programming world and is called the **"Hello, World!"** program.

What is the "Hello, World!" Program?

Every programmer, from beginners to experts, starts their journey by writing the same program: **"Hello, World!"** This program is like a tradition in the world of coding. It is simple but powerful because it shows you how to get the computer to display a message on the screen. In this case, we will ask the computer to say, "Hello, World!"

Think of it as introducing yourself to the computer, and the computer saying hello back to you!

Step 1: Open Your Code Editor

Before we write any code, we need to open the place where we will type our instructions—your code editor (VS Code). Let's get started:

1. Windows: Press the Windows Key, type Visual Studio Code, and open it.
2. Mac: Open your Applications folder, find Visual Studio Code, and double-click it.
3. Linux: Open your terminal and type:

```
Code
```

Then press Enter to open VS Code.

Once you have opened VS Code, you are ready to start coding!

> Fun Fact:
> Did you know that the very first "Hello, World!" program was written in 1972 by a programmer named Brian Kernighan? Since then, millions of programmers have written their own versions of "Hello, World!" in every programming language you can imagine.

Step 2: Create a New Python File

Now, we need a file to write our program in. In the programming world, files that contain Python code have a special ending: .py. This tells the computer that the file is written in Python.

1. In VS Code, click on File in the top-left corner.
2. Select New File. A blank file will appear.
3. Now we need to save this file with the correct name. Click on File again and select Save As.
4. Name the file hello.py and click Save.

Now you have a blank Python file ready to be filled with code!

Step 3: Write Your First Program

Let's write your first line of code. In your new Python file, type the following:

```
print("Hello, World!")
```

That's it! You have just written your first program! But what does it do?

- The word print is a command. It tells the computer to display something on the screen.
- The words "Hello, World!" are the message we want the computer to show.
- The quotation marks ("") tell the computer that this is text, not code.

20

When you run this program, the computer will follow your instructions and show **"Hello, World!"** on the screen.

Step 4: Run Your Python Program

Now that you've written the code, it is time to run the program and see the magic happen!

1. In VS Code, click on View at the top, then select Terminal. This will open the terminal at the bottom of the screen.
2. In the terminal, type the following command:

```
python hello.py
```

Then press Enter.

3. If everything is working correctly, you should see the message Hello, World! appear in the terminal.

Step 5: Understanding What Just Happened

Let's take a moment to understand what happened when you ran the program:

1. The Python interpreter read your code line by line.
2. It saw the command print("Hello, World!") and understood that it needed to display the message.
3. The interpreter translated this command into binary (0s and 1s) so the computer could understand it.
4. The computer followed the command and showed the message Hello, World! in the terminal.

This might seem simple, but you have just completed a huge milestone in your programming journey. You have written a program, and the computer followed your instructions!

Fun Fact:
When the first computers were built, they were so big that they filled entire rooms! Back then, running a simple program like Hello, World! would have taken up a lot of space and power. Today, you can do the same thing with just a few lines of code on a tiny laptop!

Step 6: Experiment with Your Program

Now that you know how to write and run a Python program, let's have fun! Here are a few ways you can change your program:

Change the Message:

Instead of saying **"Hello, World!"**, try saying something else: Rerun the program and see the new message.

```
print("Hello, Python!")
```

Add Another Line:

You can add more lines of code to make the program do more things. Try adding this:

Now the program will show two messages instead of one.

```
print("I am learning Python!")
```

Ask for the User's Name:

You can make the program more interactive by asking for input from the user. Try this:

When you run the program, it will ask for your name on the terminal and then greet you personally!

```
name = input("What is your name? ")
print("Hello, " + name + "!")
```

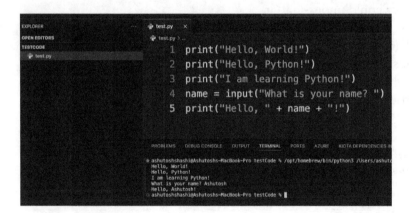

Fun Fact:
Every time you run a Python program, the computer does billions of tiny calculations in the blink of an eye. It takes all the words and symbols you have written and turns them into something it can understand instantly!

How Python Turns Your Code Into Actions

(Introduction to the Interpreter)

Now that you have written and run your first Python program, you might wonder: **How does the computer understand what I just wrote?** After all, computers do not speak English and certainly do not understand Python like we do. So, how does Python turn your code into something the computer can understand and act on? This is where the magic of the **Python interpreter** comes in!

Let's look deeper at what happens behind the scenes when you run your Python program.

The Interpreter: Your Code's Best Friend

Imagine talking to someone who speaks an entirely different language from you. To communicate, you need a **translator** who can understand both languages and explain what you are saying.

The **Python interpreter** works just like that translator!

- You: Write code in Python (English-like instructions).
- Interpreter: Translates your Python code into binary (a language the computer understands).
- Computer: Follow the translated instructions to carry out your commands.

The interpreter's job is to read each line of your code, translate it into something the computer understands, and then make sure the computer does exactly what you have asked.

How the Interpreter Works Step by Step

Let's break it down into simple steps. Every time you write and run a Python program, the interpreter does the following:

Step 1: Reading the Code

The interpreter starts by reading your Python code, line by line. It checks each line to ensure it is written correctly and follows Python's rules.

Step 2: Translating the Code

- Once the interpreter understands what each line of your code is supposed to do, it translates the Python instructions into **binary code**—a series of 0s and 1s that the computer understands.
- Computers do not understand words or sentences. They can only process **binary code** (which looks like this: 1010101001), so the

23

interpreter acts as a bridge between your code and the computer's language.

Step 3: Executing the Code

- After translating the code into binary, the interpreter sends the instructions to the computer.
- The computer follows the instructions one step at a time. In our previous example, it would print the message "Hello, World!" on the screen.

Step 4: Error Checking

- If there is a mistake in your code (like a missing quotation mark or a typo), the interpreter will stop and let you know. It is like a built-in helper that catches your mistakes and tells you what went wrong, so you can fix it.

Fun Fact:
The Python interpreter works so fast that it can translate and execute thousands of lines of code in the blink of an eye. In fact, most interpreters can process billions of instructions per second!

Interpreters vs. Compilers

You might have heard the term **compiler** before, and you might wonder how it is different from an interpreter. Both interpreters and compilers translate code into something the computer can understand, but they work a little differently.

Interpreter:
Reads your code one line at a time, translates it, and then immediately executes it. It is like giving instructions step by step.

Example:
Line 1: "Turn on the light" (Interpreter translates and executes).
Line 2: "Open the door" (Interpreter translates and executes).
The Python interpreter reads and translates your code as you run it, so if there is a mistake in the middle, it stops right away.

Compiler:
Translates the entire program into binary code **before** running anything. It processes all the instructions at once and then executes the whole program at once.

Example:
"Here's the full list of instructions: Turn on the light, open the door, and start the car." (The compiler translates all the instructions first and then runs them).

Why Python Uses an Interpreter

Python is known for being an **interpreted language**. This means that Python uses an interpreter, rather than a compiler, to run code. The benefit of this is that Python can run code almost immediately after you write it, which makes it perfect for learning and experimenting. You can write a line of code, see the result right away, and fix mistakes quickly.

Chapter 3: Understanding Python Code

Explanation of syntax and commands

What is a Programming Language?

Let's dive straight into what a **programming language** is. You already know that computers do not understand human languages like English, but they need clear instructions to perform tasks. That is where programming languages come in—they act as a bridge between us and the computer.

Why Do We Use Programming Languages?

Programming languages allow us to write commands in a way that both humans and computers can understand (with some help from the interpreter). These languages simplify complex instructions into words, symbols, and numbers that we can easily write and read.
Think of a programming language as a set of special rules that you use to give directions. Each language has its own set of rules and structure, which is known as **syntax**.

Understanding Syntax: The Rules of the Game

Every language has rules—whether it is English, French, Hindi, Spanish, or Python. In a programming language, these rules are called **syntax**. Syntax tells the computer exactly how to understand the commands you give it. For example, in Python, if you want to print a message, you must follow a specific syntax:

```
print("Hello, World!")
```

Here, print() is a command, and the text inside the quotation marks is what you want to display. If you forget a part of the syntax, like the parentheses or the quotation marks, Python will get confused and show an error.

Commands: The Actions in Python

In Python, commands are instructions that tell the computer to do something. Think of commands like actions or verbs—they make things happen in your program.

Let's look at some common Python commands:
- print(): Displays a message on the screen.
- input(): Takes input from the user.
- if: Checks if something is true or false and acts accordingly.

Here's a simple example:

```
name = input("What's your name? ")
print("Hello, " + name + "!")
```

In this example:
- input() asks the user for their name.
- print() greets the user by displaying their name on the screen.

Why Syntax and Commands Matter

Syntax ensures that the computer can interpret your commands correctly. Imagine trying to explain how to bake a cake, but leaving out the step to preheat the oven. Just like with cooking, if you leave out important steps or break the rules, the computer won't be able to complete the task correctly.

Here is an example of error

```
print("Hello, World!")
print("Hello, Python!")
print(I am learning Python!")
name = input("What is your name? ")
print("Hello, " + name + "!")
```

If you spot the error in the third line, the message's starting quote (")is missing. However, Visual Studio Code is intelligent enough to tell you there is something wrong at this line, however, if you try to run this program, you will see error on terminal like below

```
File "/Users/ashutoshshashi/testCode/test.py", line 3
    print(I am learning Python!")
                ^
SyntaxError: unterminated string literal (detected at line 3)
```

Explaining Lines of Code: What is a Function, and What is print()?

When we want the computer to do something in Python, we often use **functions**. Functions are like little helpers in programming—they carry out specific tasks for us. Think of them as pre-built tools that save us time and effort. One of Python's most commonly used functions is the **print()** function, which we have already used in our first programs!

What is a Function?

A **function** is a block of code that performs a specific task. Functions are great because they allow us to reuse code instead of writing the same instructions over and over again. Whenever you need to perform a task in Python, you can either use an existing function or create your own.
In real life, a function is like a machine. Imagine you have a cookie-making machine. Every time you press a button, it follows the same steps to bake cookies. You do not need to tell it every single step each time—it already knows what to do. Similarly, when you call a function in Python, the function knows exactly what steps to follow.

How Functions Work

Functions are like mini-programs inside your main program. You give the function a name, define what it does, and then call (or use) the function whenever you need it.
Example:
Let's say you have a function that adds two numbers together:

```
def add_numbers():
    print(2 + 3)
```

In this example:
- def add_numbers():: This line defines a function named add_numbers(). The keyword def tells Python that this is a function.
- print(2 + 3): Inside the function, Python is instructed to print the result of adding 2 and 3.
Once the function is defined, you can call it like this:

```
add_numbers()
```

When you call the function, Python knows to jump to the function's code and run the instructions inside it.

What is print()?

Now, let's look at a function we've already used: **print()**. The print() function is one of the most basic and commonly used functions in Python. Its job is simple: it displays text or other information on the screen. Whenever you want Python to show something to the user, you use the print() function. It is like Python's way of "speaking" to you. You can tell it to print messages, numbers, or even the results of calculations.
Example:

```
print("Hello, World!")
```

In this example, Python will display **"Hello, World!"** on the screen. The text inside the parentheses is called an **argument**—it's what you want the function to work with.

How Does print() Work?

When you write print(), Python takes the information inside the parentheses (like text or numbers) and sends it to the screen. It is a way of communicating with the user, showing them information, or helping you debug your program by printing useful messages.
Here are some different ways you can use print():

Print text:

```
print("Learning Python is fun!")
```

This will display: Learning Python is fun!

Print numbers:

```
print(100)
```

This will display: 100

Print the result of a calculation:

```
print(10 + 5)
```

This will display: 15

Print multiple items together:

```
name = "Alice"
print("Hello, " + name)
```

This will display: Hello, Alice

Fun Fact: The Power of print()
The print() function is like a megaphone for your program—it allows your program to "speak" to you. Programmers use print() all the time, not just to display results but also to check what is happening inside their code when they're debugging!

Creating Your Functions

You can also create your functions to make your programs easier to manage. This is especially useful when you want to perform the same task many times. Instead of writing the same code over and over, you can call your function.

Example

Let's create a function that says hello to the user:

```
def say_hello():
    print("Hello, there!")
```

Now, whenever you call say_hello(), Python will print **"Hello, there!"**.

Comments in Python (Using # to add notes to your code).

As you write more Python code, you will often want to leave yourself (or others) little notes in your program to explain what specific parts of the code do. These notes do not affect how the program runs—they are just there to help you or others understand the code better. These notes are called **comments**, and in Python, we use the # symbol to create them.

What Are Comments?

Comments are lines of text in your code that Python ignores when the program runs. They are like sticky notes you leave for yourself to explain what is happening in the code. They can be used to:
- Explain what a specific line or block of code does.
- Temporarily disable code (useful when debugging).
- Leave notes for other programmers who may read your code later.

Think of comments as little reminders or explanations that help make your code easier to understand.

Why Use Comments?

Imagine writing a program today and returning to it a few months later. Without comments, it might be hard to remember exactly why you wrote certain parts of the code the way you did. Comments act as guides to remind you of your thought process.

Also, if someone else reads your code, comments help them understand your thoughts when you wrote it. It is like writing a set of instructions for future-you or other programmers!

How to Write a Comment in Python

In Python, adding a comment is super easy. All you have to do is use the # symbol. Everything after the # on that line will be treated as a comment, and Python will ignore it when running the program.

Example:

```
# This is a comment. Python will ignore this line.
print("Hello, World!")  # This line prints a message to the screen.
```

In the example above:
- The first line is a comment: # This is a comment. Python will ignore this line.. Python skips this line entirely.
- The second line prints the message "Hello, World!" to the screen, and there is a comment after it explaining what the code does.

Where to Use Comments

1. At the Top of Your Code: Add comments at the beginning of your program to explain what the whole program does.
2. Above Complex Code: If there's a part of your code that's a bit tricky, use a comment to explain what's going on.
3. For Debugging: When debugging, you can comment out lines of code temporarily so they do not run.

Example of a Commented Program:

```
# This program asks the user for their name and greets them.

# Ask for the user's name
name = input("What is your name? ")

# Greet the user
print("Hello, " + name + "!")  # This prints a personalized greeting.
```

In this example:
- The first comment explains what the entire program does.
- The second comment explains the line that asks for the user's name.
- The third comment explains what the print statement does.

> Fun Fact: Comments Don't Affect Your Program
> You can add as many comments as you want, and it won't slow down your program or affect how it runs. Python will ignore all of them when executing the code. Comments are just there to help you stay organized!

Why Are Comments Important?

Imagine you are writing a treasure map, and you want to make sure someone else can follow it. You would leave clues along the way to explain which direction to go and what to look for. That is what comments do for your code. They act like little clues or notes to help future-you (or other programmers) navigate the code more easily.

When to Use Comments (and When Not To)

- Use comments when the code is complex or may be confusing to someone else (or yourself later on).
- Do not overuse comments in simple, straightforward code. Even if your code is easy to understand, too many comments can make it harder to read. Let your code speak for itself when possible.

Fun Fact: Python Was Named After Monty Python, Not the Snake!

When you hear the word "Python," your first thought might be of a giant, slithering snake. But did you know that the Python programming language was not named after the snake at all? It was named after a British comedy group called **Monty Python**!

The Story Behind the Name

Back in the late 1980s, a Dutch programmer named **Guido van Rossum** was working on creating a new programming language that was simple, easy to read, and fun to use. He wanted the language to have a playful name—something that did not sound too serious or intimidating.
At the time, Guido was a big fan of the **Monty Python's Flying Circus**, a popular British comedy show known for its silly and absurd humor. He enjoyed the show so much that he decided to name his new programming language after it! And that is how the programming language **Python** got its name—not from the snake, but from a comedy show that made people laugh.

Who Were Monty Python?

Monty Python was a comedy group formed in the 1960s. They became famous for their quirky and surreal sketches. They were not afraid to be weird, and their comedy often included things that did not make much sense but were still hilarious. Guido van Rossum wanted to capture this kind of fun and playful spirit with the Python language.

Monty Python's influence can even be found in some of the Python programming language's documentation, where occasional jokes and references to the comedy group exist. Python has always been about making programming accessible and enjoyable!

Why Is This Fun Fact Important?

The name Python reminds us that programming does not have to be serious all the time—it can be fun, creative, and even a little silly! Guido van Rossum wanted people to enjoy learning and using Python and chose a name that reflected that playful attitude.

So, next time you write Python code, remember that the language you are using comes from a place of humor and creativity. It is a tool to help you build amazing things, but it's also a reminder that coding can be a lot of fun!

Chapter 4: Variables – Storing Information

What Are Variables?

In Python (and most other programming languages), **variables** are one of the most important concepts you must understand. They are like containers that store information for later use in your program. But do not worry, variables are not complicated—they are simple and incredibly useful.

The Magic of Variables: Storing Information

Imagine you have a box and want to store something in it—like a toy, a snack, or a letter. Whenever you need that item, you open the box and grab it. In Python, variables work the same way. They are containers that can hold all kinds of information, such as numbers, text, or even entire lists of things.

With a variable, you give a name to a piece of information so that you can refer to it later. For example, if you want to store someone's name, you could use a variable like this:

```python
name = "Alice"
```

The variable **name** is like a box, and the value **"Alice"** is stored inside. Now, anytime you want to use the name "Alice" in your program, you refer to the variable name.

How Do Variables Work?

Variables act like placeholders for information. When you assign a value to a variable, you can use that variable anywhere in your program instead of writing the value over and over again.

Example

Let's say you want to greet a user by their name:

```
name = "Alice"
print("Hello, " + name + "!")
```

In this example:
- name = "Alice": This creates a variable called name and stores the value "Alice" inside it.
- print("Hello, " + name + "!"): This prints a greeting using the value stored in the name variable.

The great thing about variables is that you can change their values without changing the code. If you change name = "Alice" to name = "Bob", the program will greet Bob instead!

Why Are Variables Important?

Variables make your code much more flexible. Without them, you would have to write everything from scratch every time you wanted to use a different piece of information. Instead, with variables, you can just store the information once and use it whenever you need it.

Imagine you are building a video game, and you want to keep track of a player's score. You would not want to write out the player's score every single time it changes—you would use a variable to store the score and update it as the game goes on. For example:

```
score = 10
score = score + 5  # The player earns 5 more points
print("Your score is now: " + str(score))
```

Here, the variable score holds the player's current score, which you can update whenever they earn more points. Variables are so powerful because they store information that can change throughout your program!

Rules for Naming Variables

Just like naming a pet or giving your character a name in a game, you get to choose the name of your variables. But there are some simple rules to follow:
1. The name must start with a letter or an underscore (_).
2. The name can not contain spaces (you can use underscores instead, like my_variable).
3. The name can only contain letters, numbers, and underscores.
4. Variable names are case-sensitive, so Score and score are different variables.

Types of Information Stored in Variables

In Python, variables can store different kinds of information. The most common types are:
In Python, variables can store different kinds of information. The most common types are:
- Text (Strings): These are words or sentences, surrounded by quotation marks (" or '). Example: name = "Alice"
- Numbers (Integers or Floats): These are numbers, either whole numbers (integers) or numbers with decimal points (floats). Example: age = 25, temperature = 36.5
- Booleans: These are values that are either True or False. Example: is_student = True

---

Fun Fact: Why Are They Called Variables?
They are called variables because their values can vary! Just like the weather can change from sunny to rainy, the information stored in a variable can change as your program runs.

How to Create and Use Variables in Python

Now that we know the variables, it is time to learn how to create and use them in Python. Variables are straightforward, and you can create one in just a single line of code!

Creating a Variable in Python

To create a variable, you only need to choose a name for your variable, use the **equals sign (=)** to assign a value, and then write the value you want to store. Python will store this value in the variable for you to use later.

Example 1: Storing a Name in a Variable

```
name = "Alice"
```

In this example:
- **name** is the variable name.
- **=** is the assignment operator, which assigns the value to the variable.
- **"Alice"** is the value stored in the variable name.

Now, you can refer to the name variable whenever you want to use "Alice".

Using a Variable in Python

Once you have created a variable, you can use it in different parts of your program. This is especially useful when storing information like user input, calculations, or any data you need to reference later.

Example 2: Using the name Variable in a Program

```
name = "Alice"
print("Hello, " + name + "!")
```

In this example, the print() function uses the value stored in the variable name. When you run the program, Python replaces name with "Alice", and the result is:

```
Hello, Alice!
```

You can also change the value stored in a variable and use it again later in the same program.

Example 3: Changing the Value of a Variable

```
name = "Alice"
print("Hello, " + name + "!")

name = "Bob"
print("Hello, " + name + "!")
```

Here, the variable name starts with the value "Alice", but later in the program, it is changed to "Bob". The output will be:

```
Hello, Alice!
Hello, Bob!
```

Fun Fact: Python Doesn't Need You to Declare a Variable Type!
In some programming languages, you have to tell the computer what kind of data your variable will store (like text, numbers, etc.). In Python, you don't have to worry about that—Python automatically figures out the type of the variable based on the value you assign!

Updating Variables

One of the coolest things about variables is that they can be updated or changed as your program runs. You do not need to re-create the variable every time you want to change its value.

Example 4: Updating a Variable with Math

```
score = 10
score = score + 5
print("Your score is now: " + str(score))
```

In this example:
- **score = 10**: The initial value of score is 10.
- **score = score + 5**: The value of score is updated by adding 5, so now it's 15.
- **print("Your score is now: " + str(score))**: Python displays the updated score as 15.

Notice that we used **str()** function to convert the number into a string, so it can be combined with the text in the print() statement.

41

Naming Your Variables

When you create a variable, it is important to choose a name that makes sense for the data it holds. For example, calling the variable age makes sense if you're storing a person's age. If you are storing a score, calling the variable score helps you and others understand what the variable represents.

Here are some good practices for naming variables:

1. Use descriptive names: Choose names that explain what the variable is for (e.g., player_score, user_name).
2. No spaces: Use underscores (_) or capital letters to separate words (e.g., first_name, playerScore).
3. Don't start with a number: Variable names must start with a letter or an underscore.
4. Be consistent: Stick with the same style of naming throughout your program.

Naming Rules for Variables

When creating variables in Python, choosing good names is important for making your code easy to read and understand. Python has a few simple rules for naming variables, and following these rules will ensure your program runs smoothly.

Key Rules for Naming Variables

1. Variable names must start with a letter or an underscore (_).

You can start a variable with any letter from A to Z, or use an underscore, but numbers can't come first.

Examples:

```
name = "Alice"    # Correct
_score = 10       # Correct
1st_place = "Gold" # Incorrect (starts with a number)
```

2. Variable names can only contain letters, numbers, and underscores.
You can mix letters, numbers, and underscores, but you **can't use spaces** or other special characters like !, @, #, etc.

```
player_1 = "Bob"    # Correct
player-1 = "Bob"    # Incorrect (contains a dash)
```

Variable names are case-sensitive.

This means that age, Age, and AGE are all different variables in Python. Be careful with capitalization, and try to be consistent in how you name your variables.

Examples:

```
age = 20
Age = 25
AGE = 30
# These are three different variables.
```

Use descriptive names.

While Python does not stop you from using short or unclear names (like a, b, or x), it is a good idea to use names that describe what the variable holds. This makes your code easier to understand, especially if you return to it later or share it with others.

```
score = 100     # Good: Descriptive and clear
s = 100         # Not good: Vague and unclear
```

Best Practices for Variable Naming

Here are some additional tips to help you choose better variable names:
- Use underscores to separate words: This makes multi-word variable names easier to read. For example, use player_name instead of playername.
- Do not use Python keywords: Python has reserved keywords like print, if, and while that you can't use as variable names because they already have special meanings.

Examples of keywords you can not use:

```
def, return, class, if, else
```

- Be consistent: If you choose a style for naming variables (like using underscores), stick with it throughout your code. Consistency makes your program cleaner and easier to follow.

You Can Name Variables Anything (Within the Rules)

You can be creative when naming variables, as long as you follow Python's rules. Some programmers use fun or clever names for their variables, like cupcakes_left or dragon_score. Just make sure the name helps you understand what the variable is for!

Storing Different Types of Information in Variables

Now that you know how to create variables, let's explore how to use them to store different types of information. Variables can hold more than just names and ages—they can store numbers, text, and more! In this section, we will look at some practical examples of how to store and use different kinds of data in Python.

Example 1: Storing a Name (String)

A **string** is a sequence of characters, like words or sentences. You can store names, messages, or text in a string variable.

Example:

```
name = "Alice"
print("Hello, " + name + "!")
```

In this example:
- The variable name holds the string **"Alice"**.
- The print() function combines the string **"Hello, "** with the value of name to display **"Hello, Alice!"**.

Example 2: Storing an Age (Integer)

An **integer** is a whole number (without a decimal point). You can use variables to store numbers like someone's age, the number of players in a game, or a score.

Example:

```
age = 25
print("You are " + str(age) + " years old.")
```

In this example:
- The variable age stores the integer value **25**.
- Since age is a number, we need to use the str() function (provided by Python) to convert it to a string and combine it with the other text.

Example 3: Storing Decimal Values (Float)

A float is a number that has a decimal point. Floats are useful when you need to work with measurements, temperatures, or other values that aren't whole numbers.

Example:

```
temperature = 98.6
print("Your body temperature is " + str(temperature) + " degrees Fahrenheit.")
```

Here, the variable temperature holds the decimal number **98.6**, which represents a person's body temperature.
Example 4: Storing True/False Values (Boolean)
A **boolean** variable can only hold one of two values: **True** or **False**. Booleans check conditions, like whether a user is logged in or a light is on or off.

Example:

```
is_student = True
if is_student:
```

```
    print("Welcome, student!")
else:
    print("Welcome, guest!")
```

In this example:

- The variable is_student holds the boolean value **True**.
- The program checks the value of is_student to decide what message to display.

Fun Fact: How Variables Help Games Remember Your Score

Have you ever wondered how video games keep track of your score or how they remember what level you're on? It's all thanks to **variables**! Variables are like the memory banks of a game. They store important information, such as your score, health points, or even how many lives you have left, so that the game can update and show you the latest results in real-time.

How It Works: Tracking Your Score with Variables

Imagine you are playing a game where you collect coins. Each time you collect a coin, the game must add a point to your score. But how does the game remember your score? That is where variables come in.

The game uses a variable to store your score, starting at zero:

```
score = 0
```

Every time you collect a coin, the variable is updated:

```
score = score + 1
```

The game constantly updates the variable as you play. At any point, it can display your current score by using the value stored in the score variable:
print("Your score is: " + str(score))

Why Variables Are Essential for Games

Variables help games keep track of:
- **Your Score**: Every time you earn or lose points, the score variable updates.
- **Player Health**: If you lose health points in the game, the variable storing your health is updated to reflect that.
- **Inventory**: Some games let you collect items (like keys or weapons). Variables track which items you have picked up and how many you have.

Without variables, your game would not be able to remember anything! You would have to restart from the beginning every time something changed.

Example: How a Game Updates Your Score

Let's imagine a simple game where you score points by answering questions correctly. Every time you answer correctly, your score increases. Here is how the game might work with variables:

```
score = 0  # Start with a score of 0

# Player answers the first question correctly
score = score + 10
print("Your score is now: " + str(score))

# Player answers another question correctly
score = score + 5
```

```
print("Your score is now: " + str(score))
```

In this example, the score starts at 0. Each time the player answers correctly, the score variable updates and the new score is displayed.

Fun Fact: Games Rely on Variables for Everything
Not only do variables help track your score, but they also help games remember where your character is, how many lives you have, and what level you are on. Variables store everything the game needs to keep going smoothly!

Why This Matters in Bigger Games

In bigger games like **Super Mario** or **Minecraft**, variables are everywhere. They store how much health you have, how many coins you have collected, and even what items you have in your backpack. The game constantly updates these variables behind the scenes so you do not lose your progress.

Chapter 5: Data Types – The Building

Blocks of Code

What Are Data Types?

In programming, **data types** are the different kinds of information that a program can work with. Like everything in the physical world can be categorized (for example, fruits, animals, or vehicles), everything in a program belongs to a certain data type. These data types tell Python what kind of information it is dealing with, whether it is text, numbers, or even true/false values.

Think of data types as the **building blocks** of your program. They help Python know what kind of operations it can perform on a piece of data. For example, you would not add text to a number in math, just like you would not multiply your name by 5! Understanding data types is essential for writing programs that work correctly.

The Four Basic Data Types in Python

Python has four common data types that you will use frequently:

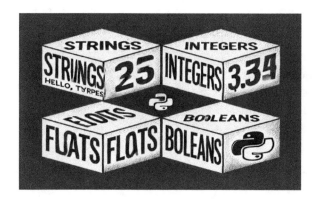

1. **Strings** (Text)
2. **Integers** (Whole Numbers)
3. **Floats** (Decimal Numbers)
4. **Booleans** (True/False)

Let's break these down one by one.

1. Strings (Text)

A string is a sequence of characters, like letters, numbers, or symbols, enclosed in quotation marks. In Python, you use either single quotes (') or double quotes (") to create a string. Strings are used to store words, sentences, or any text.

Example:

```
name = "Alice"
message = 'Hello, World!'
```

In this example, "Alice" and 'Hello, World!' are strings. You can store any text inside a string variable.

2. Integers (Whole Numbers)

An **integer** is a whole number, meaning it has no decimal point. Integers can be positive, negative, or zero, and they are used in programming for counting, scoring, and other mathematical operations.

Example:

```
age = 25
score = 100
```

Here, 25 and 100 are integers representing whole numbers.

3. Floats (Decimal Numbers)

A **float** is a number with a decimal point, like 3.14 or 98.6. Floats are used when you need more precision than whole numbers provide, such as for measurements, prices, or temperatures.

Example:

```
temperature = 98.6
price = 19.99
```

Both 98.6 and 19.99 are floats, and they represent numbers with decimals.

4. Booleans (True/False)

A **boolean** represents one of two values: **True** or **False**. Booleans are commonly used when making decisions in your program. For example, check if someone is logged in or whether a specific condition is met.

Example:

```
is_sunny = True
is_raining = False
```

In this example, the variable is_sunny holds the boolean value **True**, while is_raining holds **False**.

Why Are Data Types Important?

Data types are essential because they tell Python how to handle the information you are working with. You can not perform mathematical operations on text, and you would not use a boolean for a calculation. Each type of data behaves differently, and understanding this helps you write programs that function properly.

For example:

- You can **add** numbers (integers or floats) together, but you can't add text (strings) to a number directly.
- You can **compare** booleans to see if something is true or false, but you can't multiply them.

Fun Fact: Python Knows the Type Automatically!

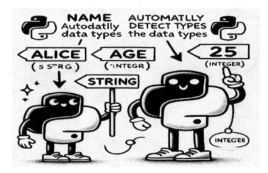

In some programming languages, you have to tell the computer what type of data you are using. But in Python, you do not need to worry about that—Python automatically knows the data type based on the value you assign!

For example:

```
age = 10    # Python knows this is an integer.
name = "Bob" # Python knows this is a string.
```

How Python Uses Data Types to Make Decisions

Python uses data types to make decisions based on the kind of information it is working with. For example, Python treats numbers, text, and True/False values differently when performing operations or comparisons. Let's explore how data types influence how Python makes decisions in your code.

Using Booleans for Decision-Making

One of the most important uses of data types in decision-making involves **booleans**. Python often uses booleans to check if something is **True** or **False**. This allows your program to make choices based on the information it has.

Example:

```
is_raining = True
if is_raining:
    print("Bring an umbrella!")
else:
    print("No need for an umbrella today.")
```

In this example, Python checks the value of is_raining. If it is **True**, the program will tell you to bring an umbrella. If it is **False**, the program will tell you that an umbrella is not needed.

Comparing Numbers and Strings

Python can also make decisions by comparing numbers and strings. For example, you can use comparison operators like >, <, ==, and != to compare values and make decisions.

Example:

```
age = 18
if age >= 18:
    print("You are an adult.")
else:
    print("You are not an adult yet.")
```

Here, Python compares the variable age to the number 18. Based on the result, it decides which message to display.
You can also compare strings in a similar way:

```
password = "python123"
if password == "python123":
    print("Access granted.")
else:
    print("Incorrect password.")
```

In this case, Python checks if the string password matches the correct password and prints the appropriate message.

Combining Data Types for Complex Decisions

You can combine different data types, like numbers and booleans, to make more complex decisions. For example, you might want to check the temperature and whether it's raining before going outside.

Example:

```
temperature = 75
is_raining = False

if temperature > 70 and not is_raining:
    print("It's a nice day for a walk!")
else:
    print("Maybe stay indoors.")
```

Here, Python makes a decision based on two conditions: the temperature and whether it is raining. If both conditions are met, the program suggests going for a walk.

Fun Fact: Python Can Handle Surprising Combinations

Did you know that you can even mix numbers and booleans in Python? For example, Python treats True as 1 and False as 0 when performing certain calculations. This can lead to some interesting results!

Example:

```
result = True + 5
print(result)  # Output: 6
```

In this example, Python treats True as 1, so the result of True + 5 is 6. This is a quirky feature that you might encounter in more advanced programs!

Example: Storing text and numbers in variables.

Now that you have learned about data types and how Python makes decisions, let's see how you store text and numbers in variables. Variables are flexible, allowing you to store different types of data, such as names, ages, or scores. This example will show how you can work with both **strings** (text) and **integers** or **floats** (numbers) in your Python programs.

Storing Text in a Variable (String)

You will use a **string to store text, such as a name or a message**. Strings are enclosed in either single (') or double (") quotation marks.

Example:

```
name = "Alice"
greeting = "Hello, " + name + "!"
print(greeting)
```

In this example:
- The variable **name** stores the string "Alice".
- The variable **greeting** combines the string "Hello, " with the value of name, creating a personalized greeting.
- The program then prints: **"Hello, Alice!"**

Storing Numbers in a Variable (Integer)

You can also store whole numbers, like ages, scores, or any other numerical data, in variables. These numbers are known as **integers**.

Example:

```
age = 25
print("You are " + str(age) + " years old.")
```

Here:
- The variable **age** stores the integer 25.
- We use **str()** to convert the number to a string so it can be combined with the text in the print statement.
- The program prints: "You are 25 years old."

Storing Decimal Numbers (Float)

If you need to store numbers with decimals, such as temperatures, prices, or measurements, you will use a **float**.

Example:

```
temperature = 98.6
print("Your body temperature is " + str(temperature) + " degrees Fahrenheit.")
```

In this example:
- The variable **temperature** holds the float value 98.6.
- The program prints: "Your body temperature is 98.6 degrees Fahrenheit."

Combining Text and Numbers

You can combine both text and numbers in your programs by converting numbers to strings using the **str()** function. This allows you to display information like someone's age or score in a sentence.

Example:

```
name = "Bob"
age = 30
print(name + " is " + str(age) + " years old.")
```

In this example:
- The variable **name** holds the string "Bob".
- The variable **age** holds the integer 30.
- The program prints: "Bob is 30 years old."

Fun Fact: You Can Store Almost Anything in a Variable!
In Python, variables can store all sorts of data, from text and numbers to lists and even entire programs. Variables make your code flexible, allowing you to reuse and update information whenever needed.

Converting Between Data Types (Casting)

In Python, data types are important because they tell the program how to handle and process the information you are working with. But sometimes, you will need to convert one data type into another. For example, you might need to turn a number into a string to print it alongside text. This process of changing one data type to another is called **casting**.

Why Convert Between Data Types?

Imagine you are writing a program that stores a person's age as a number, but you want to display it in a sentence. You must convert the number into a string since you can not directly combine text with a number. Similarly, you might want to convert a number stored as a string back into an integer to perform calculations.

Casting allows you to switch between types like:

- **String** to **Integer** or **Float** (for math operations)
- **Integer** or **Float** to **String** (for printing or displaying information)

Common Casting Functions in Python

Python provides simple functions to convert data from one type to another. Here are the most common ones:

1. **str()**: Converts data to a string (text).
2. **int()**: Converts data to an integer (whole number).
3. **float()**: Converts data to a float (decimal number).
4. **bool()**: Converts data to a boolean (True/False).

Example 1: Converting Numbers to Strings

When you want to combine a number with text, you will need to convert the number to a string using the **str()** function.

Example:

```
age = 25
print("I am " + str(age) + " years old.")
```

In this example:

- The variable age stores the number 25 (an integer).
- We use str(age) to convert the number into a string so it can be combined with the rest of the sentence.
- The program prints: **"I am 25 years old."**

Example 2: Converting Strings to Numbers

Sometimes, you will need to convert a string into a number so you can perform calculations. For this, you can use **int()** (for whole numbers) or **float()** (for decimal numbers).

Example:

```
height = "5.5"
height_in_float = float(height)  # Converts the string to a float
print(height_in_float + 1.0)     # Adds 1.0 to the height
```

In this example:
- The variable height holds the string "5.5".
- We use float(height) to convert the string into a decimal number.
- The program can now perform calculations with the height.

Example 3: Converting Numbers to Booleans

You can also convert numbers to booleans using **bool()**. In Python, 0 is treated as **False**, and any non-zero number is treated as **True**.

Example:

```
number = 10
is_positive = bool(number)  # Converts the number to a boolean
print(is_positive)          # Outputs: True
```

Here, the number 10 is converted to the boolean **True** because it is a non-zero value.

Important Notes About Casting

- If you try to convert a string that does not contain a valid number (like "hello") into an integer or float, Python will give you an error.
- When converting from float to integer, Python **drops the decimal part** without rounding. For example, int(3.99) will result in 3.

Example:

```
print(int(3.99))  # Output: 3 (decimal part is dropped)
```

Fun Fact: Python is Smart with Types

Python automatically handles data types behind the scenes, so you do not always have to worry about casting. But when you do need to convert types, Python makes it easy with simple functions like str(), int(), and float().

Fun Fact: Why Python Can Handle Numbers

Larger Than a Calculator!

Have you ever tried using a regular calculator to work with big numbers only to get an error or a strange result? That is because most calculators and even some programming languages have limits on how large the numbers they can handle are. But Python is different—it can work with numbers much **bigger** than a calculator can handle!

Why Is This Possible?

Python is designed to handle **arbitrarily large numbers**. This means you can keep adding, multiplying, or calculating with huge numbers, and Python won't give you an error (unless you run out of memory on your computer!). While calculators and some languages have fixed limits on the size of numbers, Python does not have this restriction.

How Does Python Do It?

In most calculators or programming languages, numbers are stored in a **fixed amount of space** (like 32 or 64 bits). Once you reach that limit, you can not store or calculate any larger numbers. Python, on the other hand, automatically allocates more memory to store larger numbers when needed. This flexibility is built into Python's design.

Example:

```
big_number = 99999999999999999999999999999999999999
print(big_number)
```

Python will happily print out that massive number without any problem. Most calculators would give you an error or display something like "overflow."

Python and Infinite Precision

Python is also great for handling very small numbers with many decimal places. When you're dealing with complex calculations that need high precision, Python won't cut off digits or round things prematurely. Whether it is handling the **distance between stars** or working with **scientific equations**, Python can deal with huge and tiny numbers alike!

Fun Fact: Python is Like a Super Calculator
Thanks to Python's ability to handle enormous numbers, it is like a calculator with no limits! This makes Python especially useful for scientific research, cryptography, and any other field that deals with extreme numbers.

Chapter 6: Basic Math in Python

Using Python to Do Basic Math

Python is not just great for handling text and decisions—it is also a powerful tool for doing math! You can use Python to perform basic arithmetic operations just like you would with a calculator. In fact, Python can handle all kinds of math, from simple addition and subtraction to more complex calculations. Let's explore how to use Python for basic math operations: **addition, subtraction, multiplication**, and **division**.

Addition (+)

To add two numbers in Python, you use the + symbol.

Example:

```
a = 10
b = 5
result = a + b
print(result)  # Output: 15
```

In this example:
- The variable a stores the value 10, and b stores 5.
- The expression a + b adds the two numbers together.
- Python prints the result: **15**.

Subtraction (-)

Subtraction in Python is just as easy. You use the - symbol to subtract one number from another.

Example:

```
a = 10
b = 5
result = a - b
print(result)  # Output: 5
```

Here, Python subtracts 5 from 10, and the result is **5**.

Multiplication (*)

For multiplication, Python uses the * symbol to multiply two numbers together.

Example:

```
a = 10
b = 5
result = a * b
print(result)  # Output: 50
```

In this example, Python multiplies 10 by 5, resulting in **50**.

Division (/)

In Python, you use the / symbol to divide one number by another. This operation returns a **float** (a decimal number) even if the result is a whole number.

Example:

```
a = 10
b = 5
result = a / b
print(result)  # Output: 2.0
```

Here, Python divides 10 by 5, and the result is **2.0** (a float, even though it is a whole number).

Fun Fact: Integer vs. Float Division

If you want Python to return only the whole number result of a division (without the decimal part), you can use **integer division** with the // operator.

Example:

```
a = 10
b = 3
result = a // b
print(result)  # Output: 3
```

In this case, Python divides 10 by 3 but only returns the whole number part: **3**.

Combining Operations

You can also combine these operations to perform more complex calculations. Python follows the **order of operations**, just like in math class: **parentheses** first, then **exponents**, followed by **multiplication** and **division**, and finally **addition** and **subtraction** (PEMDAS).

Example:

```
result = (10 + 5) * 2
print(result)  # Output: 30
```

Here, Python first adds 10 and 5 (because of the parentheses) and then multiplies the result by 2, giving **30**.

Creating a Simple Calculator Program

Now that you know how to perform basic math in Python, let's put that knowledge to use by creating a simple calculator program! This program will allow users to choose between different math operations (addition, subtraction, multiplication, and division) and perform calculations based on their input.

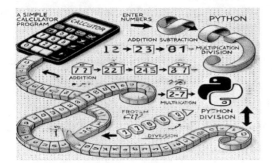

Step 1: Get User Input

To make our calculator interactive, we will ask the user to enter two numbers and choose which operation they want to perform: addition, subtraction, multiplication, or division.

Example:

```
# Ask the user to input two numbers
num1 = float(input("Enter the first number: "))
num2 = float(input("Enter the second number: "))

# Ask the user to choose an operation
operation = input("Choose an operation (+, -, *, /): ")
```

In this example:
- We use **input()** to get the numbers and the operation from the user.
- The **float()** function ensures that the user's input is treated as a number with decimals, allowing us to handle both integers and floats.

Step 2: Perform the Calculation

Next, we need to perform the calculation based on the operation the user chooses. We can use **if statements** to check which operation was selected and then perform the corresponding math operation.

Example:

```
# Perform the calculation based on the user's choice

if operation == "+":
```

```
    result = num1 + num2
elif operation == "-":
    result = num1 - num2
elif operation == "*":
    result = num1 * num2
elif operation == "/":
    result = num1 / num2
else:
    result = "Invalid operation"
```

Here:

- We use **if statements** to check the value of operation. Based on the user's choice, Python performs the correct math operation.
- If the user enters an operation that isn't one of the four valid options, the program returns **"Invalid operation"**.

Step 3: Display the Result

After performing the calculation, we want to display the result to the user.

Example:

```
# Display the result
print("The result is: " + str(result))
```

This line prints the result of the calculation. We use **str()** to convert the result (which could be a number) into a string, so it can be combined with the rest of the message.

Putting It All Together: The Simple Calculator Program
Here's the full code for the simple calculator program:

```
# Simple Calculator Program

# Step 1: Get user input
num1 = float(input("Enter the first number: "))
num2 = float(input("Enter the second number: "))
operation = input("Choose an operation (+, -, *, /): ")

# Step 2: Perform the calculation
```

```
if operation == "+":
    result = num1 + num2
elif operation == "-":
    result = num1 - num2
elif operation == "*":
    result = num1 * num2
elif operation == "/":
    result = num1 / num2
else:
    result = "Invalid operation"

# Step 3: Display the result
print("The result is: " + str(result))
```

Example Interaction with the Program

Here's what it would look like when someone runs the program:

```
Enter the first number: 10
Enter the second number: 5
Choose an operation (+, -, *, /): +
The result is: 15.0
```

In this example:
- The user enters **10** and **5** as the two numbers.
- They choose **+** as the operation, so Python adds the two numbers and displays **"The result is: 15.0"**.

Fun Fact: Your Calculator Can Handle Decimals!

By using **float()**, our calculator can handle numbers with decimals (like **5.5** or **3.14**), making it more powerful than a basic integer calculator.

```
Enter the first number: 4.2
Enter the second number: 1.8
Choose an operation (+, -, *, /): *
The result is: 7.56
```

How to Combine Numbers and Text in One Line of Code

In Python, it is common to combine **numbers** and **text** when you want to display a message that includes both. For example, you might want to print a sentence with a person's name and age or show a score in a game. However, since numbers and text are different data types, you need to use specific techniques to combine them in one line of code.

Method 1: Using str() to Convert Numbers to Strings

You first need to convert the numbers to strings to combine text and numbers. Python does not allow you to mix numbers and text directly, so you use the **str()** function to convert a number into a string, which can then be combined with other text.

Example:

```
age = 10
print("I am " + str(age) + " years old.")
```

Here:
- **age** stores the number 10.
- **str(age)** converts the number 10 to a string so it can be combined with the text "I am " and " years old.".
- The result is: "I am 10 years old."

Method 2: Using f-strings for Simpler Formatting

Python also allows you to combine numbers and text easily using **f-strings**. F-strings are a feature in Python that make it simple to embed variables (including numbers) directly into a string.

Example:

```
age = 10
print(f"I am {age} years old.")
```

In this example:
- The **f** before the string tells Python to look for variables inside the curly braces {}.
- The variable age is automatically converted to a string and inserted into the sentence.
- The result is the same as before: **"I am 10 years old."**

F-strings make it easier to combine text and variables in one line of code without manually converting the numbers using str().

Method 3: Using format() Method

Another way to combine text and numbers is by using the **format()** method. This method replaces placeholders ({}) in the string with the variables you provide.

Example:

```
age = 10
print("I am {} years old.".format(age))
```

Here:
- The curly braces {} act as placeholders for the variable age.
- The **format()** method inserts the value of age into the sentence.
- The result is: "I am 10 years old."

Fun Fact: Python is Flexible with Strings and Numbers
Thanks to str(), f-strings, and the format() method, Python gives you several ways to combine text and numbers in a single line of code. You can pick the method that you find easiest or most convenient!

Fun Fact: Python Can Do Math Faster Than a Human Can Blink!

Did you know that Python can perform calculations faster than a human blink? That is right! While it might take a few seconds to add up numbers or multiply large figures, Python can perform these calculations in a fraction of a second—sometimes in **milliseconds** or even faster!

How Fast Is Python?

A human blink takes about **100 to 400 milliseconds**, but Python can execute millions of calculations in that time. This speed is one of the reasons Python is used for scientific research, data analysis, and even artificial intelligence. When Python runs your code, it executes instructions at lightning speed, much faster than we can process information.

Why Is Python So Fast?

Python is a high-level programming language, which means it is designed to be easy for humans to write and understand. However, behind the scenes, Python uses powerful systems to convert your code into machine instructions that your computer can execute at incredible speeds.

For example:

```
result = 99999999 * 99999999
print(result)
```

Python can perform this large multiplication almost instantly and print the result, while it would take you or me much longer to calculate it by hand!

Fun Fact: Python Is Used in Fields Where Speed Matters

Because Python can handle math so quickly, it is used in fields where speed is critical, like:
- **Astronomy**: For calculating distances between stars and planets.
- **Finance**: For performing complex calculations on stock market data.
- **Physics**: For solving equations that describe how the universe works.

Chapter 7: Making Decisions – If Statements

What Are If Statements?

In Python (and many other programming languages), an **if statement** is used to make decisions in your code. It allows your program to check if a condition is true and then decide what to do based on that condition. You can think of it as the **brain** of your program—it helps the program choose between different paths or actions.

How Do If Statements Work?

An **if statement** checks a condition, which is usually a comparison or a test. If the condition is **True**, the code inside the if statement runs. If it is **False**, the program skips that section and moves on to the next part.

Think of it like this: If it is raining outside, you will bring an umbrella. If it is not raining, you won't bring one. In Python, you would write that decision like this:

Example:

```
is_raining = True

if is_raining:
    print("Bring an umbrella!")
```

In this example:
- The variable **is_raining** holds the value **True**.
- The **if statement** checks if the value of is_raining is True. Since it is, the program prints **"Bring an umbrella!"**.
- If is_raining was False, the program wouldn't print anything.

The Structure of an If Statement

An if statement has a simple structure:
1. The **if** keyword.
2. A **condition** that evaluates to either **True** or **False**.
3. A **colon (:)** to indicate the start of the code block.
4. The code block that runs if the condition is true, indented for clarity.

Example:

```
age = 18

if age >= 18:
    print("You are an adult!")
```

In this example:
- The **condition** is age >= 18, which checks if the value of age is greater than or equal to 18.
- If the condition is True, Python prints **"You are an adult!"**.

Why Are If Statements Useful?

If statements allow your program to make decisions based on the data it has. Without if statements, your program would just run the same set of instructions every time, no matter what the situation. With if statements, you can make your program smarter, allowing it to respond to different inputs or conditions.
For example:
- In a game, if the player's health is zero, the game could end.
- In an online store, if an item is in stock, the program could let the user add it to their cart.

Fun Fact!

Did you know that modern computers make millions (or even billions!) of decisions every second using if statements? Whether it's playing a video game, browsing the internet, or running a complex scientific simulation, if statements are constantly at work behind the scenes, making sure everything runs smoothly.

How to Make Decisions in Python Using If, Else, and Elif

In Python, making decisions is not just about checking one condition with an **if statement**. Sometimes, you will want to handle multiple situations and provide different outcomes depending on the result. That is where **else** and **elif** come in. Together, these tools allow your program to respond to various conditions and choose the right action for each.

If Statements: The Basic Decision

An **if statement** checks a single condition, and if that condition is true, it runs the code inside the block. If the condition is false, it skips that code.

Example:

```
age = 18

if age >= 18:
    print("You are an adult.")
```

In this example, if the variable age is **18 or higher,** Python prints **"You are an adult."** If it's less than 18, Python does nothing because there's no alternative option yet.

Else: Providing an Alternative

What if the condition is **false?** That is where **else** comes in. The **else statement** provides an alternative action when the **if** condition is not met. Think of it like a fallback option—if the condition in the **if** is false, Python will execute the **else** block.

Example:

```
age = 16

if age >= 18:
    print("You are an adult.")
else:
    print("You are not an adult yet.")
```

Here is how it works:
- If the value of age is **18 or higher**, Python will print **"You are an adult."**
- If the value of age is **less than 18**, Python will skip the **if** block and run the **else** block, printing **"You are not an adult yet."**

Elif: Handling Multiple Conditions

Sometimes you will need to check more than two conditions. This is where **elif** (short for **else if**) comes in handy. You can use **elif** to check multiple conditions one by one, allowing your program to decide between several options.

Example:

```
age = 10

if age >= 18:
  print("You are an adult.")
elif age >= 13:
  print("You are a teenager.")
else:
  print("You are a child.")
```

Here is what's happening:
- If age is 18 or higher, Python prints "You are an adult."
- If age is not 18 but is **13 or higher**, Python skips the first **if** and moves to the **elif**, printing **"You are a teenager."**
- If neither condition is met, Python runs the **else** block and prints **"You are a child."**

How If, Else, and Elif Work Together

By combining **if**, **elif**, and **else**, you can make your program handle multiple different conditions and decide which action to take for each one. Python evaluates each condition in order, and once it finds a condition that's true, it runs the corresponding code and skips the rest.

Example:

```
score = 85

if score >= 90:
    print("You got an A!")
elif score >= 80:
    print("You got a B!")
elif score >= 70:
    print("You got a C!")
else:
    print("You need to study harder.")
```

Here:
- If the score is **90 or higher**, Python prints **"You got an A!"**
- If the score is **80 to 89**, Python prints **"You got a B!"**
- If the score is **70 to 79**, Python prints **"You got a C!"**
- If none of those conditions are met, Python runs the **else** block and prints **"You need to study harder."**

Fun Fact: You Can Chain as Many Conditions as You Like!
You can use as many elif conditions as you need. This flexibility allows your program to handle a wide variety of scenarios with ease.

Example: Creating a Quiz That Gives Different Answers Based on the User's Input

Now that you know how to use **if**, **else**, and **elif** statements to make decisions in Python, let's create a fun quiz! This quiz will ask the user a question, and based on their answer, it will give a different response. We will use multiple conditions to handle different possible answers.

Step 1: Asking the Question

We will start by asking the user a simple quiz question. To do this, we will use the **input()** function to get their answer.

Example:

```
question = input("What is the capital of France? ")
```

In this example, Python will display the question and wait for the user to type their answer.

Step 2: Checking the Answer

Once the user has entered their answer, we will use an **if-elif-else** structure to check what they typed and respond accordingly. We will account for several possible answers, including correct, incorrect, and unexpected inputs.

Example:

```
if question.lower() == "paris":
    print("Correct! Paris is the capital of France.")
elif question.lower() == "london":
    print("Incorrect. London is the capital of the UK, not France.")
else:
    print("That's not the right answer. The correct answer is Paris.")
```

Here is what's happening:
- We use **question.lower()** to convert the user's input to lowercase. This makes the quiz case-insensitive (so "Paris", "paris", and "PARIS" would all be considered correct).
- If the user's answer is "paris", Python prints "Correct! Paris is the capital of France."
- If they type "london", Python prints "Incorrect. London is the capital of the UK, not France."
- If the answer is neither of these, Python prints a message saying the answer is wrong and reveals the correct answer.

Step 3: Handling Unexpected Inputs

We can extend the quiz to handle more specific wrong answers or unexpected inputs. Let's add another condition for when the user enters a completely unrelated answer.

Extended Example:

```python
if question.lower() == "paris":
    print("Correct! Paris is the capital of France.")
elif question.lower() == "london":
    print("Incorrect. London is the capital of the UK, not France.")
elif question.lower() == "rome":
    print("Nope, Rome is the capital of Italy!")
else:
    print("That's not the right answer. The correct answer is Paris.")
```

Here, we have added another **elif** condition to handle the answer **"rome"**. This gives the quiz more flexibility and allows it to handle common mistakes.

Fun Fact: You Can Make Your Quiz as Complex as You Like!
By using multiple if, elif, and else conditions, you can create quizzes with detailed responses for every possible input. You could even extend this quiz to ask multiple questions and keep track of the user's score!

Full Quiz Example:

Here is the full code for the quiz:

```python
# Simple Quiz Program

question = input("What is the capital of France? ")

if question.lower() == "paris":
    print("Correct! Paris is the capital of France.")
elif question.lower() == "london":
    print("Incorrect. London is the capital of the UK, not France.")
elif question.lower() == "rome":
    print("Nope, Rome is the capital of Italy!")
else:
```

```
print("That's not the right answer. The correct answer is Paris.")
```

Example Interaction with the Program:

Here's how the quiz might play out:

```
What is the capital of France? London
Incorrect. London is the capital of the UK, not France.
```

Or

```
What is the capital of France? Paris
Correct! Paris is the capital of France.
```

And:

```
What is the capital of France? Rome
Nope, Rome is the capital of Italy!
```

Fun Fact: Did You Know That Video Games Use If Statements to Decide What Enemies Do?

In many video games, the characters and enemies do not just act randomly—they follow a set of rules based on **if statements**! These if statements help the game decide how characters should react to different situations, making the gameplay more interactive and challenging.

How If Statements Work in Games

In video games, if statements constantly check what is happening in the game world. For example:
- If the player is nearby, an enemy might decide to attack.
- If the player is hiding, the enemy might start searching or patrolling.
- If the player is low on health, the game might show a warning or give you a health pack.

These decisions happen in real-time, and the game uses if statements to check conditions and take action.

Example in Code:

```
player_nearby = True
player_health = 20

if player_nearby:
    print("The enemy attacks!")
elif player_health < 30:
    print("The enemy backs off and waits.")
else:
    print("The enemy keeps patrolling.")
```

In this example:
- If the player is nearby, the enemy attacks.
- If the player is not nearby but has low health, the enemy might back off and wait.
- If neither condition is true, the enemy keeps patrolling the area.

If Statements Make Games Feel Alive

Without if statements, games would feel repetitive and boring. If enemies acted the same way all the time, it would be easy to predict what would happen. But games can become more dynamic and engaging by using if statements to make decisions based on player actions.
For example:
- If you sneak around quietly, enemies might not notice you.
- If you make a loud noise, enemies might come running to investigate.

Fun Fact: Complex Games Use Hundreds of If Statements
In complex video games, there are often hundreds or even thousands of if statements running in the background, constantly checking the state of the game and making decisions. These decisions can control everything from enemy behavior to the weather in the game world!

Chapter 8: Loops – Doing Things Over and Over

What Are Loops?

In Python, **loops** are used to repeat actions over and over again without having to write the same code multiple times. Imagine you want to do something a hundred times, like printing "Hello!" or counting from 1 to 100. Instead of writing one hundred lines of code, you can use a loop to **automate** the process, making your code shorter, cleaner, and more efficient.

How Do Loops Work?

A loop allows you to run a block of code **multiple times**. It keeps running the code until a certain condition is met. There are two main types of loops in Python:

1. **For Loops**: Used when you know how many times you want to repeat the action.
2. **While Loops**: Used when you want to repeat the action until a certain condition becomes false.

Think of a loop as giving Python a set of instructions and telling it to "keep going" until it finishes the job.

Example: For Loop

Let's say you want to print the numbers from 1 to 5. Instead of writing five separate print() statements, you can use a **for loop** in just a few lines of code to do the job.

Example:

```
for i in range(1, 6):
    print(i)
```

Here is what's happening:

- The loop starts at **1** and goes up to (but doesn't include) **6**.
- Python prints each number as it goes through the loop, giving the result:

```
1
2
3
4
5
```

Example: While Loop

A **while loop** repeats an action as long as a condition is **True**. This is useful when you don't know exactly how many times you will need to repeat the action, but you have a condition to stop the loop.

Example:

```
count = 1

while count <= 5:
    print(count)
    count += 1
```

Here:
- The loop keeps running as long as count is less than or equal to 5.
- After each loop, count increases by 1.
- The loop stops when count becomes greater than 5, producing the same result:

```
1
2
3
4
5
```

Why Are Loops Useful?

Loops help you save time by repeating actions without writing the same code over and over. They make your programs more efficient, especially when working with large amounts of data or performing repetitive tasks.

For example:
- **In games**: Loops can be used to repeat actions, like checking for player input or updating scores.
- **In websites**: Loops can display items like product lists or images over and over on a webpage.

Fun Fact: Loops Are Everywhere!
Almost every program you use has loops running in the background. Whether it is loading your social media feed, playing a video game, or refreshing your inbox, loops make things happen over and over without you even noticing!

How For and While Loops Work in Python

In Python, **for** and **while** loops are two powerful tools that allow you to repeat actions without writing the same code repeatedly. Both types of loops help automate tasks, but they work slightly differently. Let's take a closer look at how each one functions and when you might use them.

For Loops

A **for loop** is used when you know in advance how many times you want to repeat an action. You typically use it to iterate over a sequence, like a list of items, a range of numbers, or even characters in a string. A **for loop** goes through each item in the sequence one by one until it reaches the end.

How a For Loop Works

A for loop in Python follows this structure:

```
for item in sequence:
    # Perform some action with each item
```

The loop starts at the first item in the sequence and continues through each item, performing the specified action for each one.

Example: For Loop with a List

Let's say you have a list of fruits and you want to print each fruit's name. A for loop makes this easy:

```
fruits = ["apple", "banana", "cherry"]

for fruit in fruits:
    print(fruit)
```

Here is what happens:
- The loop starts at the first item ("apple") and prints it.
- Then it moves to "banana" and prints it.
- Finally, it prints "cherry".
- The loop stops once it has gone through all the items in the list.

Example: For Loop with a Range of Numbers

For loops are also commonly used to repeat actions with a **range of numbers**. The **range()** function is often used to generate a sequence of numbers for the loop to go through.

```
for i in range(1, 6):
    print(i)
```

Here, the loop goes through the numbers **1 to 5** and prints each one. The result is:

```
1
2
3
4
5
```

While Loops

A **while loop** is different because it does not stop after a fixed number of iterations. Instead, it keeps repeating the action as long as a certain **condition** is true. Once the condition becomes false, the loop ends. While loops are useful when you do not know in advance how many times you will need to repeat an action, but you have a condition to control when it should stop.

How a While Loop Works

A while loop in Python follows this structure:

```
while condition:
    # Perform some action
```

The loop keeps running as long as the condition is **True**. Once the condition becomes **False**, the loop stops.

Example: While Loop Counting Up

Here is an example of a while loop that counts from 1 to 5:

```
count = 1

while count <= 5:
    print(count)
    count += 1
```

In this example:
- The loop starts with count set to **1**.
- The loop checks if count <= 5. If it is, the loop prints the current value of count and then adds 1 to it.
- The loop continues until count is no longer less than or equal to 5, at which point it stops.

The result is the same as the for loop example:

```
1
2
3
4
5
```

Differences Between For and While Loops

- **For Loops**: Best when you know in advance how many times you want to repeat an action. Typically used with sequences like lists, ranges, or strings.

- **While Loops**: Best when you don't know how many times the loop will run but you have a condition that will eventually become false. While loops give more flexibility but require careful control to avoid **infinite loops** (loops that never stop).

Example: Infinite Loop

If you forget to update the condition in a while loop, it could run forever!

```
while True:
    print("This loop will run forever unless you stop it!")
```

This loop has no stopping condition and will continue forever unless interrupted.

Fun Fact: Loops Are Like Robots Repeating Tasks!
Imagine a robot that keeps watering plants until all the plants are done. That is like a for loop! Now imagine a robot that keeps watering plants until the soil is wet enough. That is more like a while loop!

Example: Counting from 1 to 10 Using a Loop

In Python, you can use a **for loop** or a **while loop** to count from 1 to 10. Both loops can get the job done, but they work slightly differently. Let's look at how to use each loop type to accomplish this simple task.

Using a For Loop to Count from 1 to 10

The **for loop** is perfect when you know exactly how many times you want to repeat something—in this case, 10 times. You can use Python's **range()** function to generate numbers from 1 to 10, and the for loop will go through each one.

Example:

```
for i in range(1, 11):
    print(i)
```

Here is what's happening:
- The **range(1, 11)** generates numbers starting from **1** and goes up to, but doesn't include, **11**. So, it counts from 1 to 10.
- The **for loop** goes through each number and prints it.

The result is:

```
1
2
3
4
5
6
7
8
9
10
```

Using a While Loop to Count from 1 to 10

A **while loop** is a bit different. Instead of using a range of numbers, the while loop keeps running as long as a condition is true. You need to manually control when the loop stops by updating a variable inside the loop.

Example:

```
count = 1

while count <= 10:
    print(count)
    count += 1
```

Here is what's happening:
- The loop starts with the variable count set to **1**.
- The **while loop** checks if count is less than or equal to **10**. If it is, the loop prints count.
- After printing, the loop adds **1** to count using **count += 1**.
- The loop stops when count becomes greater than **10**.

The result is the same:

```
1
```

```
2
3
4
5
6
7
8
9
10
```

Which Loop Should You Use?

- **For Loop**: Use this when you know how many times you want to loop (like counting from 1 to 10). It is simpler and more straightforward in these cases.
- **While Loop**: Use this when you want the loop to continue until a certain condition is false. While loops give more flexibility, you need to be careful to update the condition, or the loop could run forever.

Fun Fact: Counting Can Be Automated with Loops!
Imagine you had to manually print the numbers from 1 to 100. That would take a lot of time! But with a loop, you can do it in just a few lines of code. Loops are great for automating repetitive tasks, saving time and reducing errors.

Fun Fact: Loops Help Your Washing Machine Keep Spinning Until Your Clothes Are Clean!

Did you know that your washing machine works just like a **loop** in programming? Like a Python loop repeats actions until a condition is met, your washing machine keeps spinning until your clothes are clean.

How Loops Work in a Washing Machine

Think about how your washing machine operates:
- It fills up with water.
- It **spins the clothes** to clean them.
- It **drains the water**, fills up again, and keeps spinning.

It does this repeatedly until your clothes are clean and rinsed. Inside the machine, there is a controller that checks whether the cleaning process is done—just like how a loop in Python keeps running until a condition becomes false.

How It is Like a While Loop

A washing machine's spinning cycle is like a **while loop** in Python. The machine keeps spinning **while** the clothes aren't clean yet. Once the clothes are clean (the condition is false), it stops spinning.

In Python:

```python
clothes_clean = False

while not clothes_clean:
    print("The machine is spinning...")
    # Eventually, the clothes get clean!
    clothes_clean = True

print("Clothes are clean!")
```

In this example:
- The **while loop** keeps going as long as the clothes aren't clean.
- Once they're clean, the loop stops and the machine is done!

Loops in Real Life

Loops aren't just for programming—they are everywhere in real life! From washing machines to microwaves, many devices use loops to repeat actions until a job is done. This is why loops are so powerful: they allow machines (and programs) to keep working automatically without needing constant input.

Fun Fact: Loops Are in More Places Than You Think
Loops are all around us! They help traffic lights change, microwaves heat food, and even make sure your favorite video game characters keep moving. Loops are like the heartbeat of many everyday technologies, making sure everything works smoothly.

Chapter 9: Lists – Storing Multiple

Things

What Are Lists in Python?

A **list** in Python is like a collection or a container that can hold multiple items in a single place. Imagine you are making a grocery list—you write down everything you need, like apples, bread, and milk, on one sheet of paper. In the same way, a Python list allows you to store multiple pieces of information in one variable.

How Lists Work

In Python, a list can store **multiple items** of any type: numbers, strings, or even other lists! Lists are useful when you need to keep track of a group of related items. Instead of creating a separate variable for each item, you can store them all in one list.

Example of a List:

```
fruits = ["apple", "banana", "cherry"]
```

Here is what's happening:
- The variable fruits is a list that contains three items: "apple", "banana", and "cherry".
- Each item in the list is separated by a **comma** and placed inside **square brackets [ ]**.

Accessing Items in a List

You can easily access any item in a list by using its **index** (its position in the list). In Python, lists are **zero-indexed**, which means the first item is at position **0**, the second at **1**, and so on.

Example:

```
print(fruits[0])  # Outputs: "apple"
print(fruits[1])  # Outputs: "banana"
```

- **fruits[0]** gives you the first item, "apple".
- **fruits[1]** gives you the second item, "banana".

Lists Can Hold Different Types of Data

Python lists are very flexible. They can store different types of data all in the same list, including numbers, strings, and even other lists!

Example:

```
mixed_list = [1, "hello", 3.14, ["a", "b", "c"]]
```

In this example:
The list mixed_list contains an integer (1), a string ("hello"), a float (3.14), and another list (["a", "b", "c"])!

Why Use Lists?

Lists are incredibly useful because they allow you to:
- **Group related items**: Store all the fruits you need to buy, the students in your class, or the high scores in a game.
- **Organize data**: Instead of creating multiple variables, you can store everything in one place and access items by their position.
- **Easily manipulate data**: You can add, remove, or change items in a list with just a few commands.

Fun Fact: Lists Are Like Shopping Baskets!
Think of a Python list like a shopping basket at the grocery store. You can add multiple items to the basket (just like adding items to a list), and you can remove items when you no longer need them. Python helps you keep everything organized, just like a basket keeps your groceries in one place.

How to Create and Use Lists

Lists are one of the most important and versatile tools in Python. They allow you to store multiple items in a single variable and access them easily whenever needed. In this section, we will learn how to create a list, add items to it, and use lists in practical ways.

Creating a List

To create a list in Python, you use **square brackets** [ ] and separate the items inside with **commas**. You can store strings, numbers, or any other data type in a list. Here is how to create a simple list:

Example:

```
fruits = ["apple", "banana", "cherry"]
```

In this example, the list fruits contains three items: "apple", "banana", and "cherry". You can think of a list as a box where you can store multiple pieces of information.

Accessing Items in a List

Each item in a list has an **index** (its position in the list), and Python allows you to access these items using the index. Lists are **zero-indexed**, meaning the first item is at index **0**, the second at index **1**, and so on.

```
print(fruits[0]) # Outputs: "apple"
print(fruits[1]) # Outputs: "banana"
```

In this example:
- **fruits[0]** gives you the first item in the list, "apple".
- **fruits[1]** gives you the second item, "banana".

Adding Items to a List

You can add new items to a list using the **append()** function. This function adds the new item to the **end** of the list.

Example:

```
fruits.append("orange")
print(fruits)  # Outputs: ['apple', 'banana', 'cherry', 'orange']
```

Here is what happens:
- **fruits.append("orange")** adds "orange" to the end of the fruits list.
- Now, the list contains four items: "apple", "banana", "cherry", and "orange".

Changing an Item in a List

You can also **change** an item in a list by assigning a new value to its index.

Example:

```
fruits[1] = "blueberry"
print(fruits)  # Outputs: ['apple', 'blueberry', 'cherry']
```

In this example:
- The item at index **1** (which was "banana") is changed to "blueberry".
- The list is now: ['apple', 'blueberry', 'cherry'].

Removing Items from a List

You can remove items from a list using the **remove()** function. This function removes the first occurrence of the specified item.

Example:

```
fruits.remove("cherry")
print(fruits)  # Outputs: ['apple', 'banana']
```

Here, the item "cherry" is removed from the list, leaving only "apple" and "banana".

Looping Through a List

You can use a **for loop** to go through each item in a list and perform actions with them. This is useful when you want to repeat an action for every item in the list.

Example:

```
for fruit in fruits:
    print(fruit)
```

This loop will print each fruit in the list:

```
apple
banana
cherry
```

Why Use Lists?

Lists are great because they allow you to store and manipulate multiple pieces of information at once. Whether you're keeping track of your shopping list, game scores, or a group of student names, lists let you organize and manage data efficiently.

Fun Fact: Lists Are Like Toolboxes!
Imagine a toolbox where you can store different tools. You might have a hammer, a screwdriver, and a wrench all in one place. A Python list works the same way—you can store multiple items (tools) in one container (the list), making it easy to access and use them when needed.

Example: Storing a List of Favorite Foods

Let's create a Python list to store a collection of your favorite foods! Lists make it easy to store multiple related items in one place, so instead of creating separate variables for each food, we can store them all in a single list.

Step 1: Create the List

To begin, let's create a list of some favorite foods. We'll use square brackets [ ] and separate each food item with a comma.

Example:

```
favorite_foods = ["pizza", "sushi", "ice cream", "tacos", "pasta"]
```

In this example:
- The variable **favorite_foods** stores a list of five items: "pizza", "sushi", "ice cream", "tacos", and "pasta".
- Each item is a **string** and represents a favorite food.

Step 2: Access the Foods in the List

You can access any food in the list by using its **index**. Lists are **zero-indexed**, meaning the first item is at position **0**.

Example:

```
print(favorite_foods[0]) # Outputs: "pizza"
print(favorite_foods[2]) # Outputs: "ice cream"
```

In this example:
- **favorite_foods[0]** gives you the first food in the list, which is "pizza".
- **favorite_foods[2]** gives you the third food in the list, "ice cream".

Step 3: Add a New Favorite Food

Let's say you have discovered a new favorite food—**"burgers"**. You can easily add it to the list using the **append()** function.

Example:

```
favorite_foods.append("burgers")
print(favorite_foods) # Outputs: ['pizza', 'sushi', 'ice cream', 'tacos', 'pasta', 'burgers']
```

Here, "burgers" is added to the end of the list, and now the list contains six favorite foods.

Step 4: Change a Food Item

You might change your mind about one of your favorite foods. Maybe you no longer like **"tacos"** and want to replace it with **"salad"**. You can change any item in the list by assigning a new value to its index.

Example:

```
favorite_foods[3] = "salad"
print(favorite_foods)  # Outputs: ['pizza', 'sushi', 'ice cream', 'salad', 'pasta', 'burgers']
```

In this example, the item at index **3** (which was "tacos") is replaced with "salad".

Step 5: Remove a Food Item

If you want to remove a food from your list, you can use the **remove()** function. Let's remove **"pasta"** from the list.

Example:

```
favorite_foods.remove("pasta")
print(favorite_foods)  # Outputs: ['pizza', 'sushi', 'ice cream', 'salad', 'burgers']
```

Here, "pasta" is removed from the list, and now the list has five items again.

Looping Through the List

You can also use a **for loop** to go through each food in the list and print it.

Example:

```
for food in favorite_foods:
    print(food)
```

This loop will print each food item in the list:

```
pizza
sushi
ice cream
salad
burgers
```

Fun Fact: Lists Are Like Your Favorite Recipe Book!
Imagine your favorite recipe book. Each recipe is stored neatly in the book, and you can access any recipe just by flipping to the right page. A Python list works the same way—you can store all your favorite foods (or any other items) in a list and access them easily.

Adding, Removing, and Changing Items in a List

Python lists are dynamic, meaning you can easily add, remove, or change items after you've created them. This flexibility makes lists a powerful tool for organizing and managing data in your programs.

Adding Items to a List

You can add items to a list using the **append()** function, which adds an item to the **end** of the list. If you want to insert an item at a specific position, you can use the **insert()** function.

Adding to the End with append()

The **append()** function is the simplest way to add a new item to the end of a list.

Example:

```
fruits = ["apple", "banana", "cherry"]
fruits.append("orange")
print(fruits)  # Outputs: ['apple', 'banana', 'cherry', 'orange']
```

Here:

- **fruits.append("orange")** adds "orange" to the end of the list.
- The new list is: ['apple', 'banana', 'cherry', 'orange'].

Inserting at a Specific Position with insert()

The **insert()** function allows you to add an item at a specific index in the list.

Example:

```
fruits = ["apple", "banana", "cherry"]
fruits.insert(1, "blueberry")
print(fruits)  # Outputs: ['apple', 'blueberry', 'banana', 'cherry']
```

In this case:
- **fruits.insert(1, "blueberry")** inserts "blueberry" at index **1**.
- The new list is: ['apple', 'blueberry', 'banana', 'cherry'].

Removing Items from a List

You can remove items from a list using the **remove()** function or the **pop()** function.

Removing by Value with remove()

The **remove()** function removes the first occurrence of the specified value.

Example:

```
fruits = ["apple", "banana", "cherry"]
fruits.remove("banana")
print(fruits)  # Outputs: ['apple', 'cherry']
```

Here:
- **fruits.remove("banana")** removes "banana" from the list.
- The new list is: ['apple', 'cherry'].

Removing by Index with pop()

The **pop()** function removes an item at a specific index. If no index is provided, it removes the last item in the list.

Example:

```
fruits = ["apple", "banana", "cherry"]
fruits.pop(2)
print(fruits)  # Outputs: ['apple', 'banana']
```

In this example:
- **fruits.pop(2)** removes the item at index **2**, which is "cherry".
- The new list is: ['apple', 'banana'].

If you don't provide an index, pop() will remove the last item in the list by default:

```
fruits.pop()  # Removes the last item, "banana"
```

Changing Items in a List

You can change an item in a list by assigning a new value to its **index**.

Example:

```
fruits = ["apple", "banana", "cherry"]
fruits[1] = "blueberry"
print(fruits)  # Outputs: ['apple', 'blueberry', 'cherry']
```

Here:
- **fruits[1] = "blueberry"** replaces the item at index **1** (which was "banana") with "blueberry".
- The new list is: ['apple', 'blueberry', 'cherry'].

Why This Is Useful

The ability to add, remove, and change items in a list gives you a lot of flexibility when managing data. Whether you are building a to-do list, tracking game scores, or managing a group of student names, Python lists allow you to dynamically adjust the contents based on your needs.

Fun Fact: Lists Are Like a Dynamic Party Invitation!
Imagine sending out party invitations. You can add more people (like using append()), remove people who can't make it (like using remove()), or replace a guest with someone else (like assigning a new value to an index). Python lists make it easy to manage your guest list dynamically!

Fun Fact: Python Can Store Millions of Items in a List in the Blink of an Eye!

Did you know that Python is incredibly fast at managing lists? It can store and handle **millions** of items in a list in just a fraction of a second! Whether you are storing thousands of names, numbers, or even complex data, Python lists are designed to be quick and efficient.

How Fast Is Python with Lists?

Python lists are dynamic, meaning you can keep adding items without worrying about hitting a limit. Behind the scenes, Python is optimized to manage lists, making it possible to store and manipulate huge amounts of data—like millions of items—very quickly.

For example, you can easily create a list with **millions** of numbers like this:

```
big_list = list(range(1, 1000001))
print(len(big_list))  # Outputs: 1000000
```

Here:
- Python creates a list of numbers from **1 to 1,000,000** in a split second.
- The **len()** function confirms that the list contains exactly **1,000,000** items.

Why Is Python So Fast with Lists?

Python uses a powerful system behind the scenes to manage memory efficiently. When you add an item to a list, Python does not just store that item—it also prepares space for more items, so when you need to add even more, it can do so quickly without slowing down.

Fun Fact: Lists in Big Data and AI
Python's ability to handle massive lists is one reason it's so popular in fields like big data and artificial intelligence. Researchers and data scientists use Python to analyze huge datasets with millions of rows of information. Python lists make it easy to process and manage all this data at lightning speed.

Chapter 10: Dictionaries – Storing Information with Keys

What Are Dictionaries in Python?

A **dictionary** in Python is a collection of data where each item is stored as a **key-value pair**. It is similar to a real-world dictionary where you have a word (the key) and its definition (the value). Instead of just storing a list of items like a Python list, dictionaries allow you to assign specific **keys** to each **value**, making it easy to look up information based on those keys.

How Do Dictionaries Work?

In a Python dictionary, you store information as **key-value pairs**. The **key** is used to describe or label the **value**, which can be any data type, like numbers, strings, or even other collections (lists, dictionaries, etc.).

Example of a Dictionary:

```python
person = {
    "name": "Alice",
    "age": 25,
    "city": "New York"
}
```

In this example:
- **"name"** is the key, and **"Alice"** is the value.
- **"age"** is the key, and **25"** is the value.
- **"city"** is the key, and **"New York"** is the value.

You can think of a dictionary as a more advanced list, where each value is labeled with a key, making it easy to access specific data.

Accessing Values in a Dictionary

To access a value in a dictionary, you use the key associated with that value. Instead of using an index like in lists, you use the key to look up its corresponding value.

Example:

```
print(person["name"])  # Outputs: "Alice"
print(person["age"])   # Outputs: 25
```

Here:
- **person["name"]** gives you the value "Alice".
- **person["age"]** gives you the value 25.

Why Use Dictionaries?

Dictionaries are especially useful when you want to store and organize information that has a label or a description. They're great for storing structured data, like information about a person, a product, or any kind of record. Here are some real-world uses for dictionaries:
- **Storing user profiles** with details like name, email, and age.
- **Organizing product details**, such as price, description, and stock quantity.
- **Mapping categories** or tags to content in a website or app.

Dictionaries vs. Lists

- **Lists**: Store items in a specific order, and you access items using their index (position in the list).
- **Dictionaries**: Store items as key-value pairs, and you access items using a key, which gives more flexibility since you don't need to remember an index.

Example:
- In a list, you might have to remember that "Alice" is in position 0, and 25 is in position 1.
- In a dictionary, you can use **"name"** to get "Alice" and **"age"** to get 25, making the code more readable and meaningful.

Fun Fact: Dictionaries Are Like Real-Life Dictionaries!

Just like a real dictionary where you look up a word (key) to find its definition (value), Python dictionaries work the same way. You use the key to quickly find the value you're looking for. This makes dictionaries perfect for storing and retrieving information efficiently.

How to Create and Use Dictionaries

Dictionaries in Python are incredibly useful for storing and organizing information as key-value pairs. You can create a dictionary with keys (like labels) and values (the actual data). In this section, we will learn how to create a dictionary, access and modify its values, and add or remove items from it.

Creating a Dictionary

You can create a dictionary using curly braces { } and separating keys from values with a **colon :**. A comma separates each key-value pair.

Example:

```
student = {
    "name": "John",
    "age": 18,
    "grade": "A"
}
```

In this example:
- The dictionary **student** has three key-value pairs.
  - **Key**: "name", **Value**: "John"
  - **Key**: "age", **Value**: 18
  - **Key**: "grade", **Value**: "A"

Accessing Values in a Dictionary

To access the values stored in a dictionary, you use the **key**. This is like looking up a word in a real dictionary to find its definition.

Example:

```
print(student["name"])  # Outputs: "John"
```

```
print(student["age"])  # Outputs: 18
```

Here:
- **student["name"]** retrieves the value associated with the key "name", which is "John".
- **student["age"]** retrieves the value associated with the key "age", which is 18.

Adding Items to a Dictionary

You can add a new key-value pair to an existing dictionary by assigning a value to a new key.

Example:

```
student["school"] = "Greenwood High"
print(student)
# Outputs: {'name': 'John', 'age': 18, 'grade': 'A', 'school': 'Greenwood High'}
```

Here:
- A new key-value pair is added: "school": "Greenwood High".
- The dictionary now has four key-value pairs.

Changing Values in a Dictionary

You can change the value associated with a key by reassigning a new value to that key.

Example:

```
student["grade"] = "A+"
print(student)  # Outputs: {'name': 'John', 'age': 18, 'grade': 'A+', 'school': 'Greenwood High'}
```

In this example, the value of the "grade" key is updated from "A" to "A+".

Removing Items from a Dictionary

You can remove key-value pairs from a dictionary using the **pop()** function. This function removes the key and its associated value.

Example:

```
student.pop("age")
print(student) # Outputs: {'name': 'John', 'grade': 'A+', 'school': 'Greenwood High'}
```

Here:
- The key "age" and its value 18 are removed from the dictionary.
- The updated dictionary no longer contains the "age" key.

Looping Through a Dictionary

You can use a **for loop** to go through a dictionary and access each key or value. You can loop over just the keys, just the values, or both.

Example: Looping Over Keys:

```
for key in student:
    print(key) # Outputs: name, grade, school
```

Example: Looping Over Values:

```
for value in student.values():
    print(value) # Outputs: John, A+, Greenwood High
```

Example: Looping Over Key-Value Pairs:

```
for key, value in student.items():
    print(f"{key}: {value}")
# Outputs:
# name: John
```

```
# grade: A+
# school: Greenwood High
```

Why Use Dictionaries?

Dictionaries are great for:
- **Storing structured data**: They allow you to store information in a more organized way than lists, especially when you need to label the data.
- **Quick access**: You can look up a value using a key, which makes it faster and more readable than remembering a list index.
- **Flexibility**: You can add, remove, and change data on the fly without much effort.

Fun Fact: Dictionaries Are Like Real-Life Address Books!
Think of a Python dictionary like an address book. You can store a person's name (key) and their phone number (value). You look up the name (key) to find the phone number (value). Similarly, dictionaries help you store and retrieve information efficiently in your Python programs.

Example: Storing Information About People (Name, Age, Favorite Color)

Dictionaries are perfect for storing detailed information about people, such as their name, age, and favorite color. In this example, we will create a dictionary for one person and then expand it to store information about multiple people.

Step 1: Creating a Dictionary for One Person

Let's start by creating a dictionary that stores information about one person: their name, age, and favorite color. Each piece of information will be stored as a **key-value pair** in the dictionary.

Example:

```
person = {
  "name": "Alice",
  "age": 30,
```

```
    "favorite_color": "blue"
}
```

In this example:
- **"name"** is the key, and **"Alice"** is the value.
- **"age"** is the key, and **30"** is the value.
- **"favorite_color"** is the key, and **"blue"** is the value.

You can easily access this information using the keys:

```
print(person["name"])  # Outputs: "Alice"
print(person["age"])   # Outputs: 30
print(person["favorite_color"])  # Outputs: "blue"
```

Step 2: Adding More People

Now, let's expand this example to store information about multiple people. We can do this by creating a **dictionary of dictionaries**, where each person has their own dictionary inside a larger dictionary.

Example:

```
people = {
    "person1": {
        "name": "Alice",
        "age": 30,
        "favorite_color": "blue"
    },
    "person2": {
        "name": "Bob",
        "age": 25,
        "favorite_color": "green"
    },
    "person3": {
        "name": "Charlie",
        "age": 35,
        "favorite_color": "red"
    }
}
```

Here is what's happening:
- **people** is a dictionary that contains multiple dictionaries, one for each person.
    - **"person1"** is the dictionary for Alice.
    - **"person2"** is the dictionary for Bob.
    - **"person3"** is the dictionary for Charlie.

Now, you can access the information about each person using their key:

```
print(people["person1"]["name"])  # Outputs: "Alice"
print(people["person2"]["age"])   # Outputs: 25
print(people["person3"]["favorite_color"])  # Outputs: "red"
```

Step 3: Adding New People

You can add new people to the people dictionary by creating a new dictionary for them and assigning it to a new key.

Example:

```
people["person4"] = {
    "name": "Diana",
    "age": 28,
    "favorite_color": "purple"
}

print(people["person4"])  # Outputs: {'name': 'Diana', 'age': 28, 'favorite_color': 'purple'}
```

In this example:
- A new person, Diana, is added to the people dictionary with her own set of information (name, age, favorite color).
- The dictionary now stores information about four people.

Step 4: Modifying Information

You can also update the information about a person by accessing their dictionary and changing the value of a key.

Example:

```
people["person2"]["age"] = 26
print(people["person2"]["age"])  # Outputs: 26
```

In this example:
Bob's age is updated from 25 to 26 by modifying the "age" key in his dictionary.

Step 5: Removing a Person

If you no longer need to store information about a person, you can remove their entry from the dictionary using the **pop()** function.

Example:

```
people.pop("person3")
print(people)  # Outputs: Dictionary without Charlie's information
```

In this example:
Charlie's entire dictionary is removed from the people dictionary.

Fun Fact: Dictionaries Are Like a Filing Cabinet!
Imagine a filing cabinet with folders for each person. Inside each folder, you have information like their name, age, and favorite color. A Python dictionary works the same way: each key (like "person1") is like a folder, and the values inside are the information about that person.

Adding, Removing, and Accessing Information in Dictionaries

Dictionaries in Python are incredibly flexible. You can add new key-value pairs, access existing information, and remove items from a dictionary as needed. This makes them ideal for storing and organizing data that you need to manipulate dynamically.

Adding Information to a Dictionary

To add a new key-value pair to a dictionary, you can assign a value to a new key. If the key already exists, its value will be updated; if it doesn't exist, it will be added to the dictionary.

Example: Adding a New Key-Value Pair

```python
person = {
    "name": "Alice",
    "age": 30
}

# Add a new key-value pair
person["favorite_color"] = "blue"
print(person)
# Outputs: {'name': 'Alice', 'age': 30, 'favorite_color': 'blue'}
```

Here:
- The dictionary person originally contains two key-value pairs.
- **person["favorite_color"] = "blue"** adds a new key ("favorite_color") with the value "blue" to the dictionary.

Accessing Information in a Dictionary

To access a value in a dictionary, you use the **key** associated with that value. If you try to access a key that does not exist, Python will raise a **KeyError** unless you use the get() method, which allows for safe access.

Example: Accessing Values

```python
person = {
    "name": "Alice",
    "age": 30,
    "favorite_color": "blue"
}

# Access values using their keys
print(person["name"])  # Outputs: "Alice"
```

```
print(person["age"])  # Outputs: 30
```

If you are unsure whether a key exists, you can use the **get()** function, which will return None (or a default value you specify) if the key doesn't exist.

Example: Using get() to Safely Access Keys

```
print(person.get("hobby", "No hobby found"))  # Outputs: "No hobby found"
```

In this case:
The key "hobby" doesn't exist in the person dictionary, so get() returns the default message "No hobby found".

Removing Information from a Dictionary

You can remove key-value pairs from a dictionary using the **pop()** function or the **del** keyword. Both methods allow you to remove an item by its key.

Example: Removing with pop()

```
person = {
    "name": "Alice",
    "age": 30,
    "favorite_color": "blue"
}

# Remove a key-value pair using pop()
person.pop("age")
print(person)  # Outputs: {'name': 'Alice', 'favorite_color': 'blue'}
```

Here:
The key "age" and its value 30 are removed from the dictionary using the pop() function.

113

Example: Removing with del

```
del person["favorite_color"]
print(person)  # Outputs: {'name': 'Alice'}
```

In this example:
The key "favorite_color" is removed using the **del** keyword.

Modifying Information in a Dictionary

If you want to update or change a value in a dictionary, you can assign a new value to an existing key.

Example: Modifying a Value

```
person["age"] = 31
print(person)  # Outputs: {'name': 'Alice', 'age': 31}
```

Here:
The value of the "age" key is updated from 30 to 31.

Why This Is Useful

Adding, removing, and modifying items in a dictionary gives you the flexibility to store and manipulate data dynamically. Whether you're building a database of users, managing a product catalog, or keeping track of scores in a game, Python dictionaries provide a fast and efficient way to handle structured data.

Fun Fact: Dictionaries Are Like a Flexible Whiteboard!
Imagine a whiteboard where you can write down people's names, their ages, and their favorite colors. If someone changes their favorite color, you can easily erase it and write a new one. If a new person joins, you can add their information to the board. This is exactly how Python dictionaries work—they let you add, remove, and update information with ease.

Fun Fact: Python Dictionaries Work Just Like a Real-Life Dictionary, Matching Words to Meanings!

Python dictionaries are similar to the dictionaries you use to look up words in real life! In a real-life dictionary, you have **words** (the **keys**) and their **meanings** (the **values**). Just like you use a real dictionary to look up the meaning of a word, in Python, you use keys to look up values.

How Does This Work in Python?

In a Python dictionary, each **key** is like a word, and each **value** is like the definition of that word. You can think of Python dictionaries as a quick way to match information, just like a real dictionary matches words to meanings.

Example:

```
dictionary = {
    "apple": "A sweet fruit",
    "banana": "A yellow fruit",
    "python": "A programming language"
}

# Accessing the meaning of 'apple'
print(dictionary["apple"])  # Outputs: "A sweet fruit"
```

Here:
The key "apple" is like looking up the word "apple" in a real dictionary, and its value "A sweet fruit" is the definition you get in return.

Why Is This So Useful?

Just like a real dictionary helps you quickly find the meaning of a word, Python dictionaries help you quickly access specific information by using a key. This makes it easy to organize and retrieve data without having to search through long lists or multiple variables.

115

For example, in a game, you might have a dictionary of player stats:

```
player_stats = {
    "health": 100,
    "armor": 75,
    "experience": 1200
}

# Accessing the player's health
print(player_stats["health"])  # Outputs: 100
```

The key "health" lets you directly access the player's health without needing to remember any specific position or index.

Dictionaries in Real Life

Think of all the things you could store in a Python dictionary:
- A phone book matching **names** to **phone numbers**.
- A glossary matching **terms** to their **definitions**.
- A product catalog matching **item names** to their **prices**.

The concept is simple yet powerful, and it is used in Python to help store and retrieve structured data quickly and efficiently.

Fun Fact: Real-Life Dictionary Comparison
Imagine flipping through a real-life dictionary. You look up a word (the key), and the dictionary gives you its meaning (the value). Python dictionaries work the same way: when you provide the key, Python gives you the associated value instantly. This makes Python dictionaries fast and efficient, especially when dealing with large amounts of data!

Chapter 11: Tuples – Storing Information That Can't Be Changed

What Are Tuples?

A **tuple** in Python is a collection of items that are ordered and unchangeable. Once you create a tuple, you can not add, remove, or change the items inside it. Tuples are written with **parentheses ( )** instead of square brackets like lists.

Creating a Tuple

You create a tuple by placing items inside parentheses ( ), separated by commas. The items can be any data type, just like in lists.

Example:

```
my_tuple = ("apple", "banana", "cherry")
print(my_tuple)
```

In this example, my_tuple contains three items: "apple", "banana", and "cherry".

Accessing Items in a Tuple

You can access items in a tuple by referring to their **index**, just like in lists. Tuples are **zero-indexed**, meaning the first item is at position **0**.

Example:

```
print(my_tuple[0])  # Outputs: "apple"
print(my_tuple[1])  # Outputs: "banana"
```

Why Use Tuples?

You might be wondering why you would use a tuple instead of a list. Here are a few reasons:

- **Data Integrity**: If you have data that shouldn't be changed, like dates or fixed coordinates, a tuple ensures that the data stays the same.
- **Faster Access**: Tuples are slightly faster than lists because they are immutable (unchangeable).
- **Safer Storage**: You can be sure that the data stored in a tuple won't be accidentally modified in your program.

> Fun Fact: Tuples Are Like Locked Boxes!
> Think of a tuple like a box that you can open and look inside, but once the box is sealed, you can not change anything inside it. This makes tuples perfect for storing things you do not want to change, like coordinates on a map or dates on a calendar.

How to Create and Use Tuples

Now that you know what tuples are and why they're useful, let's explore how to create and use them in more detail. Tuples may be immutable (unchangeable), but they are still incredibly versatile and easy to work with.

Creating a Tuple

To create a tuple, place items inside **parentheses ( )**, separated by commas. You can include any data type in a tuple, including strings, numbers, and other tuples.

Example:

```
fruit_tuple = ("apple", "banana", "cherry")
```

In this example, **fruit_tuple** contains three items: "apple", "banana", and "cherry". The items in a tuple are ordered, just like in lists.

Empty Tuple:

You can also create an empty tuple with just parentheses:

```
empty_tuple = ()
```

Accessing Tuple Items

You access items in a tuple just like you do with lists—using **indexes**. Tuples are **zero-indexed**, so the first item is at index 0, the second item is at index 1, and so on.

Example:

```
print(fruit_tuple[0])  # Outputs: "apple"
print(fruit_tuple[2])  # Outputs: "cherry"
```

In this example:
- **fruit_tuple[0]** gives you the first item, "apple".
- **fruit_tuple[2]** gives you the third item, "cherry".

Slicing Tuples

You can **slice** a tuple to access a range of items. Slicing works by specifying a start and end index, and Python will return a new tuple with the selected items.

Example:

```
print(fruit_tuple[0:2])  # Outputs: ('apple', 'banana')
```

In this example:
fruit_tuple[0:2] returns the first two items, "apple" and "banana". The slice goes from index 0 up to, but not including, index 2.

Immutability of Tuples

Once you create a tuple, you **cannot** modify it. This means you cannot add, remove, or change any items in the tuple. If you try to change an item, Python will raise an error.

Example:

```
fruit_tuple[0] = "orange"  # This will raise an error!
```
119

In this case, Python will give an error because you're trying to change the value of an item in the tuple, which is not allowed.

Combining Tuples

Although you can not modify a tuple, you can create a **new tuple** by combining existing ones. This does not change the original tuples; it simply creates a new one.

Example:

```
fruit_tuple = ("apple", "banana", "cherry")
veg_tuple = ("carrot", "potato")
combined_tuple = fruit_tuple + veg_tuple
print(combined_tuple)
# Outputs: ('apple', 'banana', 'cherry', 'carrot', 'potato')
```

In this example, we combine the two tuples into a new one called **combined_tuple**.

Tuple Length

You can find out how many items are in a tuple using the **len()** function.

Example:

```
print(len(fruit_tuple))  # Outputs: 3
```

In this case, the tuple **fruit_tuple** contains three items, so **len(fruit_tuple)** returns 3.

Why Use Tuples?

Here is a quick recap of why tuples are useful:
- **Immutability**: Tuples are great for storing data that shouldn't change, like dates, coordinates, or configuration settings.

- **Faster access**: Since tuples can't be modified, Python can access them faster than lists.
- **Data integrity**: You can ensure that your data remains unchanged throughout your program by using tuples instead of lists.

Fun Fact: Tuples Are Like Frozen Pizza!
Think of a tuple like a frozen pizza. Once the pizza is made and frozen, you can't change the toppings or remove any ingredients—it stays exactly as it was. In the same way, once you create a tuple, its contents are fixed. You can access and use the pizza (tuple), but you can't change it!

Advanced Uses of Tuples

Now that you know how to create and use basic tuples, let's dive into some of the more advanced features of tuples. We will explore how to nest tuples, use tuples in functions, and give some practical examples of where tuples really shine.

Nesting Tuples

You can nest tuples inside other tuples, just like you can with lists. This is useful for organizing more complex data structures, where each tuple represents a group of related items.

Example:

```
nested_tuple = (("apple", "banana"), ("carrot", "potato"), ("pizza", "pasta"))
print(nested_tuple[0])  # Outputs: ('apple', 'banana')
print(nested_tuple[1][1])  # Outputs: 'potato'
```

In this example:
- **nested_tuple[0]** gives you the first tuple, ("apple", "banana").
- **nested_tuple[1][1]** drills down to the second item of the second tuple, which is "potato".

Nesting allows you to create layers of information, making it easier to organize related data within a single tuple.

Using Tuples in Functions

Tuples are often used in functions, especially when you need to return multiple values. Because tuples are immutable, they're a safe way to return multiple pieces of data without the risk of them being accidentally modified.

Example: Returning Multiple Values from a Function

```
def get_person_info():
    name = "Alice"
    age = 30
    favorite_color = "blue"
    return name, age, favorite_color

# Unpack the returned tuple
person_info = get_person_info()
print(person_info)  # Outputs: ('Alice', 30, 'blue')
```

In this example, the function **get_person_info()** returns a tuple containing three pieces of information: a name, an age, and a favorite color. This tuple is then stored in the variable **person_info**.

Unpacking Tuples

You can **unpack** the values in a tuple into separate variables. This is particularly useful when working with functions that return multiple values.

```
name, age, favorite_color = get_person_info()
print(name)  # Outputs: "Alice"
print(age)   # Outputs: 30
print(favorite_color)  # Outputs: "blue"
```

In this case:
- The tuple returned by **get_person_info()** is unpacked into three separate variables: **name, age,** and **favorite_color**.
- This makes it easy to work with individual values from a tuple.

Converting Between Tuples and Lists

Although tuples are immutable, you can convert them into lists if you need to modify the contents. You can also convert lists into tuples if you want to make their contents immutable.

Example: Converting a Tuple to a List

```
fruit_tuple = ("apple", "banana", "cherry")
fruit_list = list(fruit_tuple) # Convert to a list
fruit_list.append("orange") # Add an item
print(fruit_list) # Outputs: ['apple', 'banana', 'cherry', 'orange']
```

In this example, the tuple **fruit_tuple** is converted into a list so that we can add an item to it. Once you've made the necessary changes, you can convert it back into a tuple if needed.

Example: Converting a List to a Tuple

```
fruit_list = ["apple", "banana", "cherry"]
fruit_tuple = tuple(fruit_list)  # Convert to a tuple
print(fruit_tuple) # Outputs: ('apple', 'banana', 'cherry')
```

This process allows you to switch between mutable lists and immutable tuples, depending on your program's requirements.

When to Use Tuples vs. Lists

- Use Tuples when:
  - You have data that should not change.
  - You want faster access to data.
  - You're working with **function arguments** or **return values** that should remain constant.
- Use Lists when:
  - You need to modify, add, or remove items frequently.
  - You're working with data that can change over time.

Real-World Examples of Tuples in Action

Tuples might seem simple, but they are incredibly useful in real-world
scenarios. They are often used when working with data that shouldn't be
modified, for performance improvements, or when returning multiple
values from functions. This section will look at some real-world examples
where tuples shine.

Example 1: Storing Coordinates

One common use of tuples is to store **coordinates** like latitude and
longitude. Since coordinates typically do not change, a tuple is the perfect
choice for storing this data.

Example:

```
coordinates = (40.7128, -74.0060)  # Latitude and longitude of New York City
print(coordinates)  # Outputs: (40.7128, -74.0060)
```

Here:
The tuple **coordinates** stores the latitude and longitude of New York City.
Since coordinates are constant, using a tuple ensures that this data remains
unchangeable.

Example 2: Returning Multiple Values from Functions

Tuples are often used in functions that need to return multiple values. This
allows you to return several pieces of information at once without having
to use multiple return statements or complex data structures.

Example:

```
def calculate_rectangle_area_and_perimeter(length, width):
    area = length * width
    perimeter = 2 * (length + width)
```

```
    return area, perimeter  # Returning a tuple with both values

# Unpack the returned values
area, perimeter = calculate_rectangle_area_and_perimeter(5, 3)
print(f"Area: {area}, Perimeter: {perimeter}")
```

In this example:
- The function **calculate_rectangle_area_and_perimeter()** calculates both the area and perimeter of a rectangle.
- It returns these two values as a tuple, which is then **unpacked** into the variables area and perimeter.

Example 3: Using Tuples as Dictionary Keys

Dictionaries in Python require their keys to be **immutable**. Since tuples are immutable, they can be used as dictionary keys, unlike lists. This is useful when you need to create dictionaries with composite keys.

Example:

```
locations = {
    (40.7128, -74.0060): "New York City",
    (34.0522, -118.2437): "Los Angeles",
    (51.5074, -0.1278): "London"
}

print(locations[(40.7128, -74.0060)])  # Outputs: "New York City"
```

In this case:
- Each **key** in the locations dictionary is a tuple that represents the latitude and longitude of a city.
- You can use these tuple keys to look up the city's name in the dictionary.

Example 4: Swapping Values Using Tuples

Tuples provide a simple and elegant way to swap the values of two variables without needing a temporary variable.

Example:

```
a = 10
b = 20

# Swap the values
a, b = b, a
print(a, b)  # Outputs: 20 10
```

Here:
Using tuple unpacking, the values of a and b are swapped in a single line. This is much cleaner and more efficient than using a temporary variable.

Example 5: Tuples in For Loops

Tuples can also be used in **for loops** when iterating over sequences that contain multiple items. This is often seen when working with lists of tuples or dictionaries.

Example:

```
students = [("Alice", 90), ("Bob", 85), ("Charlie", 95)]

for name, score in students:
    print(f"{name}: {score}")
```

In this example:
- The list **students** contains tuples, where each tuple holds a student's name and their score.
- In the **for loop**, the tuple is unpacked so that name and score can be accessed directly.

When Tuples Shine in Real-World Projects

- **Coordinates and Fixed Data**: Tuples are great for storing data you don't want to accidentally change, like coordinates, dates, and configuration settings.

- **Function Returns**: Tuples make it easy to return multiple values from functions, allowing you to pass back related data in a simple, immutable format.
- **Performance**: Since tuples are immutable, they have a slight performance advantage over lists. This makes them a good choice when you are working with large datasets or performance-critical applications.
- **Safe Keys**: Use tuples as dictionary keys when you need a reliable, unchangeable key.

Fun Fact: Tuples Are Used in Databases!
In the world of databases, a row of data is often called a tuple because it represents a fixed set of values, like a record of information. Just like in Python, tuples in databases can store related data in an ordered, unchangeable format!

Chapter 12: Functions – Python's Superpowers

What Are Functions?

A **function** in Python is like a **mini-program** within your main program. It is a reusable block of code that performs a specific task. Functions allow you to break down your code into smaller, manageable pieces, which makes your code easier to read, understand, and maintain. By using functions, you can avoid repeating the same code multiple times and make your programs more organized.

Why Use Functions?

Imagine you are writing a long story, and you have to describe the same action (like "opening a door") several times. Instead of writing out the entire description each time, it would not be easier if you could say, "The door was opened," and the reader already knows what that means. Functions work the same way in your code.

Functions help you:
1. **Reuse Code**: Write a function once and use it anywhere in your program.
2. **Organize Code**: Break down complex tasks into smaller steps, each handled by a function.
3. **Avoid Repetition**: If you find yourself writing the same code multiple times, you can put it in a function and call that function whenever needed.

How Do Functions Work?

Python defines a function using the **def** keyword, followed by the function name and parentheses ().
Example:

```
def greet():
    print("Hello, World!")
```

In this example, we define a function called **greet()** that simply prints "Hello, World!". This function doesn't take any inputs, and it does not return anything. It just performs the task of printing a message.

Calling a Function

Once you have defined a function, you can **call** it (or **invoke** it) to run the code inside.
Example:

```
greet()  # Outputs: Hello, World!
```

Here, we call the **greet()** function, and it performs its task by printing "Hello, World!".

Why Do Functions Matter?

Let's say you are writing a game, and the character needs to jump multiple times throughout the game. Instead of writing the same code for the jump action over and over again, you can create a function called **jump()** and call it whenever the character needs to jump. This makes your code more efficient and easier to update. If you ever want to change how the jump works, you only need to update the **jump()** function.

Parts of a Function

A Python function typically has three main parts:
1. **Function Definition**: This is where you define the function, including its name and what it does.
2. **Function Parameters**: These are optional values you can pass into the function when calling it (we'll cover this in the next section).
3. **Function Call**: This is where you tell the program to actually run the function.

Fun Fact: Functions Are Like Recipes!
Think of a function as a recipe. Once you write down a recipe for making cookies, you can follow that recipe anytime you want to make cookies. Similarly, once you define a function, you can call it anytime to perform a task without having to rewrite the steps.

How to Create Your Own Functions in Python

Creating your own functions in Python is simple and powerful. Functions let you break down tasks into reusable blocks of code, making your programs more organized and efficient. In this section, we'll walk through how to create your own functions step by step.

Step 1: Defining a Function

To create a function in Python, you use the **def** keyword, followed by the name of the function and parentheses (). After that, you write the code that the function should execute, indented underneath the function definition.
Example:

```
def say_hello():
    print("Hello, everyone!")
```

Here is what's happening:
- **def** tells Python you are defining a function.
- **say_hello** is the name of the function.
- The code indented below the function prints "Hello, everyone!" when the function is called.

Step 2: Calling a Function

Once you have defined a function, you can **call** it whenever you want to run the code inside it. To call a function, simply type its name followed by parentheses ().

Example:

```
say_hello()  # Outputs: Hello, everyone!
```

In this example, when you call the **say_hello()** function, it prints the message "Hello, everyone!".

Step 3: Adding Parameters to a Function

Functions become even more powerful when they can accept **parameters**. Parameters are values that you can pass into a function to customize what it does. You define parameters inside the parentheses of the function definition.

Example:

```
def greet(name):
  print(f"Hello, {name}!")
```

In this example:
- **name** is the parameter that the function **greet()** accepts.
- When you call the function, you provide a value for **name**, and the function will print a personalized greeting.

Calling the Function with a Parameter:

```
greet("Alice")  # Outputs: Hello, Alice!
greet("Bob")   # Outputs: Hello, Bob!
```

Here, you can see how the function changes based on the value you pass to the **name** parameter.

Step 4: Returning Values from a Function

Sometimes, you want your function to perform a calculation or operation and then **return** a value that you can use later in your program. To do this, you use the **return** keyword.

Example:

```
def add_numbers(a, b):
  return a + b
```

In this example:

- **a** and **b** are the parameters that the function **add_numbers()** accepts.
- The function adds these two numbers together and returns the result.

Calling the Function and Using the Returned Value:

```
result = add_numbers(5, 3)
print(result)  # Outputs: 8
```

Here, the function **add_numbers(5, 3)** returns the value 8, which is stored in the variable **result**.

Step 5: Using Default Parameter Values

You can also give parameters **default values** in your function definition. This means that if the user does not provide a value, the function will use the default.

Example:

```
def greet(name="friend"):
    print(f"Hello, {name}!")
```

In this case:
- The function **greet()** has a default value of "friend" for the **name** parameter.
- If you don't provide a name when calling the function, it will use the default value.

Calling the Function with and without a Parameter:

```
greet("Alice")  # Outputs: Hello, Alice!
greet()         # Outputs: Hello, friend!
```

Why Create Your Own Functions?

Creating your own functions allows you to:

133

- **Reuse code**: Write a function once and use it multiple times.
- **Make your code cleaner**: Functions help you organize your code into logical blocks, making it easier to read and maintain.
- **Customize behavior**: By using parameters, you can make your functions flexible and adaptable to different needs.

> Fun Fact: Functions Are Like Custom Tools!
> Imagine you're building a toolbox. Each tool in your toolbox is like a function you've created—it performs a specific task and can be reused whenever needed. By creating your own functions, you're essentially building a set of custom tools that you can use in any project.

Example: Writing a Function to Calculate the Area of a Rectangle

Let's dive into a practical example by creating a function to calculate the **area of a rectangle**. This example will show you how to use function parameters to accept inputs and how to return a value that you can use elsewhere in your program.

Step 1: Define the Function

To calculate the area of a rectangle, we need two pieces of information: the **length** and the **width**. We can create a function called **calculate_area()** that takes these two values as parameters.

Function Definition:

```
def calculate_area(length, width):
    area = length * width
    return area
```

Here is what's happening:
- **def calculate_area(length, width)**: We define the function with two parameters, length and width.
- **area = length * width**: The function multiplies the length and width to find the area of the rectangle.
- **return area**: The function returns the calculated area so that we can use it later.

Step 2: Calling the Function

Now that we have defined the function, let's call it and provide the values for the length and width of the rectangle.

Example of Calling the Function:

```
rectangle_area = calculate_area(5, 3)
print(f"The area of the rectangle is: {rectangle_area}")
```

In this example:
- We call the **calculate_area(5, 3)** function, passing in the values 5 (length) and 3 (width).
- The function calculates the area as **5 * 3 = 15** and returns the result.
- The result is stored in the variable **rectangle_area**, which is then printed.

Output:

```
The area of the rectangle is: 15
```

Step 3: Using the Function with Different Values

You can reuse the **calculate_area()** function with different values for the length and width. This is the power of functions—they allow you to reuse the same code for different inputs.

Example:

```
area1 = calculate_area(10, 2)
area2 = calculate_area(7, 4)

print(f"Area 1: {area1}")  # Outputs: Area 1: 20
print(f"Area 2: {area2}")  # Outputs: Area 2: 28
```

In this example, the function calculates the area of two rectangles:

- **Rectangle 1** has a length of 10 and a width of 2, resulting in an area of **20**.
- **Rectangle 2** has a length of 7 and a width of 4, resulting in an area of **28**.

Step 4: Adding Default Values

We can make the function even more flexible by adding **default values** for the length and width. This way, if the user doesn't provide any values, the function will use the default values.

Function with Default Values:

```
def calculate_area(length=1, width=1):
    area = length * width
    return area
```

Now, if you call the function without providing values, it will use the default values of 1 for both length and width.

Example:

```
default_area = calculate_area()
print(f"Default area: {default_area}")  # Outputs: Default area: 1
```

In this case, the function calculates the area using the default values, so the result is **1** (1 * 1).

Why This Example Matters

This example demonstrates how functions can make your code more efficient, reusable, and easier to maintain. Instead of writing the code to calculate the area of a rectangle multiple times, you can write the function once and call it whenever you need it. This approach also makes your code more flexible, as you can easily change the length and width without modifying the function itself.

Fun Fact: Functions Are Like Math Formulas!

Think of a function like a math formula. Once you have the formula for calculating the area of a rectangle (length * width), you can use that formula over and over again with different numbers. Similarly, you can use the calculate_area() function with different inputs to get the area of any rectangle.

Reusing Functions to Make Your Code Cleaner

One of the greatest benefits of functions is that they allow you to **reuse code**. Instead of writing the same block of code over and over again, you can define a function once and call it whenever you need it. This makes your code more efficient, cleaner, and easier to maintain.

Why Reuse Functions?

When you write large programs, you often encounter situations where you must perform the same task multiple times. Without functions, you would have to write the same code repeatedly. This not only makes your program longer and harder to read, but it also increases the chances of making mistakes.

By using functions, you:

1. **Reduce Repetition**: You write the code once and reuse it whenever needed.
2. **Increase Readability**: Your code becomes easier to understand because it's broken into smaller, manageable functions.
3. **Simplify Maintenance**: If you need to update the logic, you only need to change the function definition once, and it will apply everywhere you've used that function.

Example: Reusing a Function

Let's take the **rectangle area** function from the previous example and see how reusing it can make your code cleaner.

Without Functions (Repetitive Code)

Imagine you want to calculate the area of three different rectangles. Without functions, you would have to write the same formula multiple times:

```
# Rectangle 1
length1 = 5
```

```
width1 = 3
area1 = length1 * width1
print(f"Area of rectangle 1: {area1}")

# Rectangle 2
length2 = 7
width2 = 4
area2 = length2 * width2
print(f"Area of rectangle 2: {area2}")

# Rectangle 3
length3 = 6
width3 = 2
area3 = length3 * width3
print(f"Area of rectangle 3: {area3}")
```

This approach is repetitive, and if you had more rectangles, the code would get longer and harder to manage.

With Functions (Cleaner Code)

By using the **calculate_area()** function, you can simplify the code and make it reusable:

```
def calculate_area(length, width):
    return length * width

# Reusing the function for multiple rectangles
area1 = calculate_area(5, 3)
area2 = calculate_area(7, 4)
area3 = calculate_area(6, 2)

print(f"Area of rectangle 1: {area1}")
print(f"Area of rectangle 2: {area2}")
print(f"Area of rectangle 3: {area3}")
```

Here, the **calculate_area()** function is reused for all three rectangles. This approach is much cleaner and easier to maintain. If you needed to change how the area is calculated (for example, to add a special condition), you would only have to update the function itself, not every instance where you calculate the area.

Reusing Functions with Different Parameters

Functions are flexible because they can accept different parameters. This means you can reuse the same function to handle different inputs, making it highly adaptable.

Example: Reusing a Function with Different Values

Let's write a simple function that greets people by name.

```
def greet(name):
    print(f"Hello, {name}!")
```

Now, instead of writing a greeting for each person individually, you can call the **greet()** function with different names:

```
greet("Alice")
greet("Bob")
greet("Charlie")
```

Outputs:

```
Hello, Alice!
Hello, Bob!
Hello, Charlie!
```

By reusing the **greet()** function, you avoid writing the same print statement over and over again. This makes your code more efficient and reduces repetition.

Why Does Reusing Functions Matter?

Reusing functions leads to:
1. **Less Code**: Your program becomes shorter because you don't need to repeat the same code multiple times.

139

2. **More Flexibility**: You can use the same function with different inputs, which makes your code adaptable to different situations.
3. **Easier Updates**: If you need to change the function's behavior, you can do so in one place, and the changes will apply everywhere that function is used.

Fun Fact: Reusing Functions Is Like Baking Cookies!
Imagine you're baking cookies. Instead of mixing the ingredients from scratch every time, you can use the same recipe over and over to make as many batches as you want. Functions are like recipes for your code—they let you follow the same steps multiple times without having to rewrite them from scratch.

Fun Fact: Functions Help Programs Like Google Run Faster by Breaking Down Big Tasks into Small Ones

Did you know that giant programs like Google, YouTube, and Facebook rely on functions to run efficiently? Functions allow these large, complex systems to break down enormous tasks into smaller, more manageable pieces. This makes the programs faster and easier to maintain, even when millions of people are using them simultaneously.

How Functions Make Big Programs Faster

Imagine trying to write a program that handles all of Google's search requests at once—it would be incredibly overwhelming! Instead of tackling the entire task as one big block of code, engineers break the task down into smaller functions that handle individual parts, like finding the right web pages, displaying the results, and managing user preferences. Each function has its own specific job, making the overall system more organized and efficient.

How Does It Work?

When you search for something on Google, several functions are working behind the scenes to:
1. **Take Your Search Query**: A function processes the words you typed into the search box.

2. **Find Results**: Another function looks through Google's massive index of web pages to find the best matches.
3. **Rank the Results**: A different function ranks the results to show you the most relevant information first.
4. **Display the Results**: A final function handles how the results are displayed on your screen.

By dividing these tasks into smaller functions, Google can handle millions of searches at once without slowing down.

Why Breaking Down Tasks Is Important

Functions make big programs faster because:

*   **Parallel Processing**: Different functions can run simultaneously, allowing multiple tasks to be completed simultaneously.
*   **Efficiency**: Functions only run when needed, so the program doesn't waste time doing unnecessary work.
*   **Modularity**: Breaking a big task into smaller functions makes updating and fixing specific parts of the program easier without affecting the entire system.

Real-Life Comparison: Assembly Line

Think of a factory assembly line. Instead of one person building an entire car, each worker handles a specific part of the process, like attaching the wheels or painting the car. This makes the production process faster and more efficient.

Functions work the same way in programming. Each function handles a small, specific task, forming a complete, efficient system.

Fun Fact: Google's Functions Are Like Tiny Robots!
Imagine Google as a giant team of tiny robots, each responsible for a specific task. One robot grabs the search results, another arranges them, and yet another makes sure they look good on your screen. These "robots" are like functions—they all work together to make Google run fast and smoothly.

Chapter 13: Working with Libraries

What Are Python Libraries?

Python libraries are **pre-written collections of code** that you can use in your own programs to make development faster and easier. Think of libraries as **toolkits** full of useful functions, classes, and modules already written by other developers. Instead of writing everything from scratch, you can use a library to handle specific tasks like working with data, creating graphics, or building websites.

Why Use Libraries?

Python libraries save time and effort by providing **ready-made solutions** for common tasks. You don't have to reinvent the wheel when writing a program. For example, if you want to create graphs, instead of writing code to handle all the drawing and layout yourself, you can use a library like **Matplotlib** that already provides functions for generating beautiful charts and graphs.

Here is why Python libraries are so helpful:

1. **Save Time**: Libraries let you focus on the unique parts of your project while using pre-built tools for common tasks.
2. **Avoid Errors**: By using tried-and-tested code from libraries, you reduce the chances of bugs and errors.
3. **Access Specialized Tools**: Libraries give you access to advanced tools and functions that would be difficult or time-consuming to create on your own.
4. **Collaborate and Share**: Many libraries are open-source, meaning that developers around the world collaborate to improve and share these libraries with the Python community.

Types of Libraries in Python

Python has thousands of libraries, each designed to handle specific tasks. Some libraries are built into Python, while others can be installed as needed.

Built-in Libraries:

These libraries come with Python, so you don't need to install anything extra to use them. Some common built-in libraries include:

- **math**: Provides mathematical functions like square roots, trigonometry, and more.
- **random**: Helps you generate random numbers, which is useful in games or simulations.
- **datetime**: Makes it easy to work with dates and times.

External Libraries:

These libraries are not included with Python by default, but you can install them using a package manager like **pip**. Some popular external libraries include:

- **numpy**: Used for working with large sets of numbers and doing complex mathematical calculations.
- **pandas**: Great for data analysis and manipulating tables of data.
- **matplotlib**: Helps you create graphs and charts to visualize data.
- **requests**: Allows you to interact with the web and download data from websites.

How Do Libraries Work?

Libraries are made up of **modules**, which are files of Python code that can be imported into your program. Each module contains functions, classes, and variables that you can use to perform specific tasks.

To use a library in your program, you need to **import** it. This tells Python to include the code from the library in your script.

Example: Using the math Library

```
import math

# Using the math library to calculate the square root of 16
result = math.sqrt(16)
print(result)  # Outputs: 4.0
```

In this example:
- **import math** tells Python to include the math library in your program.

- We then use the **math.sqrt()** function to calculate the square root of 16.

How to Install External Libraries

Many Python libraries are not included by default, but you can easily install them using **pip**, Python's package manager. For example, if you want to install the **requests** library to work with web data, you would run this command in your terminal or command prompt:
pip install requests
Once installed, you can import and use the library just like a built-in library.

> Fun Fact: Libraries Are Like Toolboxes!
> Imagine a Python library as a toolbox. Instead of having to create your own hammer, screwdriver, or wrench, you can simply open the toolbox and grab the tools you need. Python libraries work the same way—they provide ready-made tools that you can use to build your program without starting from scratch.

How to Import and Use Libraries in Python

Python makes it incredibly easy to use libraries in your programs. Libraries contain pre-written code that you can **import** and use, which saves you time and effort. In this section, we'll walk through how to import both built-in and external libraries, and how to use them in your Python programs.

Step 1: Importing a Library

The first step in using a Python library is to **import** it into your program. This tells Python to load the library's code so that you can use its functions and tools.

Syntax:

```
import library_name
```

Example: Using the math Library

Let's say you want to use the built-in **math** library to perform some mathematical calculations.

```
import math

# Using math to calculate the square root of 25
result = math.sqrt(25)
print(result)  # Outputs: 5.0
```

In this example:
- **import math** loads the math library.
- You can then use the functions inside math, like **math.sqrt()** to calculate square roots.

Step 2: Importing Specific Functions or Modules

Sometimes, you might not need everything in a library. Instead of importing the entire library, you can import specific **functions** or **modules**.

Syntax:

```
from library_name import specific_function
```

Example: Importing Only the sqrt Function from math

```
from math import sqrt

# Using the sqrt function without referencing the whole library
result = sqrt(36)
print(result)  # Outputs: 6.0
```

In this example:
from math import sqrt imports only the **sqrt()** function from the math library, allowing you to use it directly without the math. prefix.

Step 3: Using Aliases for Libraries

Sometimes library names can be long, or you might want to shorten them for convenience. Python allows you to assign an **alias** to a library or module when you import it.

Syntax:

```
import library_name as alias
```

Example: Giving numpy an Alias

```
import numpy as np

# Using numpy functions with the alias 'np'
array = np.array([1, 2, 3, 4])
print(array)
```

In this example:
import numpy as np gives the numpy library the shorter alias np, so you can refer to it more easily in your code.

Step 4: Installing and Importing External Libraries

In addition to built-in libraries, Python has a huge collection of **external libraries** that you can install using **pip**. Once installed, you can import them just like any built-in library.

Installing a Library Using Pip:

To install an external library, open your terminal or command prompt and type:

```
pip install library_name
```

For example, to install the **requests** library for handling web requests, you would run:

```
pip install requests
```

Once installed, you can import and use it in your code:
Example: Using the requests Library

```
import requests

# Sending a GET request to a website
response = requests.get("<https://www.example.com>")
print(response.status_code)  # Outputs: 200 (which means the request was
successful)
```

In this example:
- **import requests** loads the requests library.
- You can then use it to send web requests, like **requests.get()**, to download data from the internet.

Combining Multiple Libraries

You can import and use multiple libraries in the same program. This allows you to combine different tools and functions to solve more complex tasks.
Example: Using math and random Together

```
import math
import random

# Generate a random number and find its square root
random_number = random.randint(1, 100)
square_root = math.sqrt(random_number)

print(f"Random number: {random_number}, Square root: {square_root}")
```

In this example:
- The **random** library is used to generate a random number between 1 and 100.
- The **math** library is used to calculate the square root of that random number.

Organizing Imports

When importing libraries in a Python program, it is a good practice to list all of your imports at the **top of your script**. This helps keep your code organized and easy to read.

Example: Importing Multiple Libraries

```
import math
import random
import datetime
```

By organizing your imports at the beginning of your file, you make it clear which libraries your program depends on.

```
Fun Fact: Importing Libraries Is Like Shopping for Ingredients!
Imagine you're baking a cake, and you need ingredients like flour, sugar, and eggs.
Instead of growing your own ingredients, you go to the store and buy them. In Python,
libraries are like the ingredients for your program. You don't have to write everything
from scratch—you can import libraries that already have the tools and functions you
need!
```

Example: Using the random Library to Make a Guessing Game

Let's put what we've learned into practice by creating a simple **guessing game** using Python's random library. In this game, the computer randomly picks a number, and the player must guess what it is. We will use the random library to generate the secret number and write the game logic using functions and conditionals.

Step 1: Import the random Library

The random library allows us to generate random numbers, which is perfect for our guessing game. We'll use it to generate a secret number the player will try to guess.

```
import random
```

This line of code imports the random library, making its functions available for us to use in our program.

Step 2: Generate a Random Number

Next, we will use the **random.randint()** function to generate a random number between a specified range (for example, between 1 and 10). This will be the secret number the player has to guess.

```
secret_number = random.randint(1, 10)
```

This line picks a random number between 1 and 10 and stores it in the variable **secret_number.**

Step 3: Writing the Game Logic

Now let's create a loop where the player will keep guessing until they guess the correct number. We will also give the player hints if their guess is too high or too low.

```
import random

def guessing_game():
    # Step 1: Generate a random number
    secret_number = random.randint(1, 10)
    attempts = 0

    print("Welcome to the Guessing Game!")
    print("I'm thinking of a number between 1 and 10. Can you guess it?")

    while True:
        # Step 2: Get the player's guess
        guess = int(input("Enter your guess: "))
        attempts += 1

        # Step 3: Check if the guess is correct
        if guess < secret_number:
            print("Too low! Try again.")
        elif guess > secret_number:
            print("Too high! Try again.")
        else:
```

```
print(f"Congratulations! You guessed the number in {attempts} attempts.")
break
```

How the Game Works:

1. **Generate a Random Number**: The computer picks a random number between 1 and 10 using random.randint(1, 10).
2. **Player Input**: The player enters their guess, and the program compares it to the secret number.
3. **Hints**: If the guess is too low, the program prints "Too low! Try again." If the guess is too high, it prints "Too high! Try again."
4. **Win Condition**: Once the player guesses the number correctly, the game congratulates them and tells them how many attempts it took.

Step 4: Running the Game

To play the game, simply call the **guessing_game()** function in your script.

```
guessing_game()
```

When you run the program, it will prompt you to guess a number until you get it right. Here is how a sample game might look:

Sample Game Output:

```
Welcome to the Guessing Game!
I'm thinking of a number between 1 and 10. Can you guess it?
Enter your guess: 5
Too low! Try again.
Enter your guess: 8
Too high! Try again.
Enter your guess: 7
Congratulations! You guessed the number in 3 attempts.
```

Adding More Features

You can make the game more interesting by adding features like:

- **Limiting the Number of Attempts**: Let the player have only a limited number of guesses.

- **Difficulty Levels**: Increase the range of the random number for harder difficulty levels (e.g., 1 to 100).
- **Keeping Track of High Scores**: Track the fewest number of attempts it takes to guess the number correctly.

Example: Adding an Attempt Limit

```python
def guessing_game():
    secret_number = random.randint(1, 10)
    attempts = 0
    max_attempts = 5

    print("Welcome to the Guessing Game!")
    print("I'm thinking of a number between 1 and 10. You have 5 attempts to guess it.")

    while attempts < max_attempts:
        guess = int(input("Enter your guess: "))
        attempts += 1

        if guess < secret_number:
            print("Too low!")
        elif guess > secret_number:
            print("Too high!")
        else:
            print(f"Congratulations! You guessed the number in {attempts} attempts.")
            break
    else:
        print(f"Sorry, you've used all {max_attempts} attempts. The number was {secret_number}.")
```

Fun Fact: The random Library Is Used in Video Games!
Did you know that random number generators (like the ones in Python's random library) are used in video games to make things unpredictable? For example, random numbers are often used to decide what enemies appear, where items are placed, or how the game's environment changes. These random elements make games more fun and challenging!

Introduction to Common Libraries: NumPy and Matplotlib

Python has powerful libraries that can help you perform tasks ranging from data analysis to visualization. Two of the most popular and widely used libraries in the Python ecosystem are **NumPy** and **Matplotlib**. These libraries are essential for working with numerical data, performing scientific calculations, and creating visual representations of data. Let's take a closer look at what these libraries do and why they are so important.

NumPy: Working with Numerical Data

NumPy (short for **Numerical Python**) is a library that works with large numerical data sets. It provides a range of tools to perform mathematical operations on arrays (a collection of numbers or values) quickly and efficiently. NumPy is especially useful for tasks involving linear algebra, random number generation, and basic statistics. It forms the foundation of many other data science libraries like **Pandas** and **SciPy**.

Key Features of NumPy:

1. **Arrays**: The core feature of NumPy is its powerful array object, which is much more efficient than Python's built-in lists.
2. **Mathematical Operations**: You can perform fast mathematical operations on arrays, such as addition, subtraction, and matrix multiplication.
3. **Linear Algebra**: NumPy includes tools for working with matrices, solving linear equations, and performing advanced algebraic calculations.
4. **Random Numbers**: It includes functions for generating random numbers, which are useful for simulations and probability-based tasks.

Example: Creating a NumPy Array

Let's create a simple array using NumPy and perform a basic operation on it.

```
import numpy as np

# Creating a NumPy array with numbers 1 to 5
```

153

```
arr = np.array([1, 2, 3, 4, 5])

# Multiplying every element by 2
result = arr * 2
print(result)  # Outputs: [ 2  4  6  8 10 ]
```

In this example:
- **np.array()** creates a NumPy array.
- We then multiply each element in the array by 2, demonstrating how NumPy allows you to apply operations to the entire array at once.

Why Use NumPy?

- **Speed**: NumPy arrays are optimized for performance, making them much faster than regular Python lists, especially when working with large datasets.
- **Convenience**: It simplifies mathematical operations by allowing you to perform operations on entire arrays without writing loops.

Matplotlib: Visualizing Data

Matplotlib is a library used for creating **visualizations** like charts, graphs, and plots. It is one of the most popular libraries for data visualization in Python, and it works well with other libraries like **NumPy** and **Pandas**. With Matplotlib, you can create line graphs, bar charts, histograms, scatter plots, and much more. It is widely used in fields like data science, machine learning, and scientific research to help users make sense of their data through visual representation.

Key Features of Matplotlib:

1. **Plotting**: Create a wide range of 2D and 3D plots, including line plots, bar charts, pie charts, and scatter plots.
2. **Customization**: You can customize every aspect of your plots, from colors to labels, grid lines, and axes.
3. **Integration**: Matplotlib works well with other libraries like NumPy and Pandas, making it easy to plot data directly from arrays or dataframes.

Example: Creating a Simple Line Plot

Let's create a simple line plot using Matplotlib to visualize some data.

```
import matplotlib.pyplot as plt

# Sample data
x = [1, 2, 3, 4, 5]
y = [2, 4, 6, 8, 10]

# Creating a line plot
plt.plot(x, y)
plt.title("Simple Line Plot")
plt.xlabel("X-axis")
plt.ylabel("Y-axis")
plt.show()
```

In this example:
- **plt.plot(x, y)** creates a line plot with the data points x and y.
- **plt.title()**, **plt.xlabel()**, and **plt.ylabel()** add a title and labels to the plot.
- **plt.show()** displays the plot in a window.

Why Use Matplotlib?

- **Data Visualization**: Matplotlib makes it easy to visualize data, which helps you understand patterns, trends, and relationships.
- **Flexibility**: You can create everything from simple line plots to complex 3D visualizations with Matplotlib's highly customizable tools.

How NumPy and Matplotlib Work Together

NumPy and Matplotlib often go hand-in-hand when working with data. You can use NumPy to generate or manipulate numerical data, and then use Matplotlib to visualize that data in graphs or charts.

Example: Using NumPy and Matplotlib Together

Let's combine NumPy and Matplotlib to create a sine wave plot.

```
import numpy as np
import matplotlib.pyplot as plt

# Creating data using NumPy
```

155

```
x = np.linspace(0, 10, 100)  # 100 evenly spaced values between 0 and 10
y = np.sin(x)  # Sine wave values

# Plotting the sine wave using Matplotlib
plt.plot(x, y)
plt.title("Sine Wave")
plt.xlabel("X-axis")
plt.ylabel("Y-axis")
plt.show()
```

In this example:

- **np.linspace(0, 10, 100)** generates 100 evenly spaced numbers between 0 and 10 using NumPy.
- **np.sin(x)** computes the sine of each value in the array x.
- **plt.plot(x, y)** uses Matplotlib to plot the sine wave.

Fun Fact: Python's Libraries Help Power NASA and Other Big Projects!
Did you know that NumPy and Matplotlib are used in projects as complex as space exploration? Scientists and engineers at NASA use these libraries to analyze large amounts of data and visualize results from space missions. Python libraries make it possible to process and understand data on an enormous scale!

Fun Fact: Python Has a Library for Almost Everything, from Creating Games to Solving Math Problems!

One of the coolest things about Python is its vast collection of libraries—there's practically a library for every task you can imagine! Whether you want to build a video game, create a website, solve complex math problems, or even analyze data from space missions, Python has a library that can help you do it.

From Games to Graphics

Want to create your own video game? Python has libraries like **Pygame** that make it easy to build fun, interactive games. You can create characters, levels, and even add sound effects—all using just a few lines of code!

Example: Building a Game with Pygame

156

Pygame is a library that helps you create 2D games. You can use it to handle graphics, sound, and player input. With a library like Pygame, even beginners can create simple games like Snake or Tetris.

```
import pygame

# Initialize the game
pygame.init()

# Set up the game window
screen = pygame.display.set_mode((400, 300))

# Main game loop
running = True
while running:
    for event in pygame.event.get():
        if event.type == pygame.QUIT:
            running = False

pygame.quit()
```

From Art to Algorithms

Maybe you are more into creating art and graphics. Python has libraries like **Turtle**, which allows you to draw pictures and shapes by moving a virtual turtle around the screen. It's a fun and easy way to create colorful designs and introduce coding to beginners.

Python also shines when it comes to solving complex mathematical problems. Libraries like **SymPy** allow you to perform symbolic mathematics, simplifying equations, solving algebraic expressions, and even doing calculus—all through code!

Example: Solving Math with SymPy

```
import sympy as sp

# Define a variable
x = sp.symbols('x')

# Solve a simple algebraic equation
```

```
equation = sp.Eq(x**2 - 4, 0)
solution = sp.solve(equation)
print(solution)  # Outputs: [-2, 2]
```

 With **SymPy**, you can solve algebraic and calculus problems, making it a valuable tool for students and researchers.

Libraries for Almost Every Field

Python's libraries cover just about every field you can think of:

- **Data Science**: Libraries like **Pandas** and **NumPy** allow you to manipulate, analyze, and visualize huge datasets.
- **Web Development**: Frameworks like **Django** and **Flask** make building websites fast and efficient.
- **Artificial Intelligence**: Libraries like **TensorFlow** and **PyTorch** help developers build AI models and neural networks for machine learning projects.
- **Astronomy and Physics**: Tools like **AstroPy** allow scientists to analyze astronomical data and simulate celestial events.

Why Are Python Libraries So Powerful?

Libraries are powerful because they save you time and effort. Instead of writing code from scratch, you can rely on the work of other developers who have created these useful tools. You simply install the library, import it into your project, and start using it. This allows you to focus on solving your specific problem, without worrying about the technical details behind the scenes.

Fun Fact: Python Has Over 300,000 Libraries!
Python has a library for almost everything, and the Python Package Index (PyPI) hosts more than 300,000 different libraries. From building robots to predicting the weather, there's a Python library for nearly any project you can imagine!

Chapter 14: Reading and Writing Files

How to Read from a File in Python

One of the most important tasks in programming is working with files. Whether you're reading data from a text file, loading configuration settings, or processing large datasets, Python makes it easy to handle files with just a few lines of code. This section will explore how to **read from a file** using Python.

Step 1: Opening a File

Before you can read from a file, you need to **open** it. Python provides a built-in function called **open()** that allows you to open a file and specify how you want to interact with it (read, write, or append).

Syntax:

```
file_object = open("filename", "mode")
```

Here:
- **filename:** The name of the file you want to open.
- **mode:** The mode in which you want to open the file. For reading, you use "r" (which stands for **read**).

Example:

```
file = open("example.txt", "r")
```

This line of code opens the file **example.txt** in **read mode** and stores the file object in the variable **file**.

Step 2: Reading the File

Once the file is opened, you can read its contents. There are several ways to read data from a file in Python, depending on how much data you want to read at a time:

1. **Reading the Entire File**: You can read the entire file at once using the **read()** method.
2. **Reading Line by Line**: If the file has multiple lines, you can read one line at a time using **readline()** or **readlines()**.

Example: Reading the Entire File

```
file = open("example.txt", "r")
content = file.read()
print(content)
file.close()  # Always close the file after reading
```

In this example:
- **file.read()** reads the entire contents of the file and stores it in the variable **content**.
- After reading the file, it's important to **close** the file using **file.close()** to free up system resources.

Example: Reading the File Line by Line

```
file = open("example.txt", "r")

# Reading the file line by line
for line in file:
    print(line.strip())  # .strip() removes extra spaces or newlines

file.close()
```

Here:
- We use a **for** loop to go through each line in the file and print it.
- **line.strip()** is used to remove any extra spaces or newline characters.

Step 3: Using the with Statement

A better way to handle files in Python is by using the **with** statement. This automatically opens the file and closes it when you're done, even if an error occurs. This approach is safer and avoids potential issues like forgetting to close the file.

Example: Reading a File Using with

```
with open("example.txt", "r") as file:
    content = file.read()
    print(content)
```

In this example:
- **with open("example.txt", "r") as file** opens the file in read mode and assigns it to the variable **file**.
- The **with** statement automatically closes the file when the block of code is finished, so you don't need to call **file.close()**.

Handling Large Files

If you are working with a large file, it is often better to read it **line by line** to avoid loading the entire file into memory at once. This is useful when processing huge text files like logs or data exports.

Example: Efficiently Reading Large Files

```
with open("large_file.txt", "r") as file:
    for line in file:
        process_line(line)  # Replace this with your own function to handle each line
```

In this example:
We use a **for** loop inside the **with** block to process each line individually. This is more memory-efficient for large files.

Fun Fact: Python Can Read Almost Any File Format!
Did you know that Python can read not just plain text files, but also CSV files, JSON, XML, and even binary files? With the help of libraries like csv, json, and xml, Python allows you to easily process different types of files for data analysis, web development, and more.

How to Write Data to a File

Like reading from a file, Python makes writing data to a file easy. Writing files is a common task in programming, whether you want to save user input, generate reports, or store logs. This section will explore creating a file, writing data, and handling common tasks like appending data.

Step 1: Opening a File in Write Mode

To write to a file, you need to **open** it in **write mode**. Python provides different modes for writing:

- **"w"**: Write mode. If the file already exists, it will overwrite the file. If the file doesn't exist, it will create a new one.
- **"a"**: Append mode. This mode lets you add data to the end of an existing file without overwriting its contents.

Syntax:

```
file_object = open("filename", "mode")
```

- **filename**: The name of the file you want to write to.
- **mode**: Use "w" for write mode or "a" for append mode.

Example: Writing to a File

```
file = open("output.txt", "w")
file.write("Hello, World!")
file.close()  # Always close the file after writing
```

In this example:

- open("output.txt", "w") opens the file output.txt in write mode.
- **file.write("Hello, World!")** writes the string "Hello, World!" to the file.
- **file.close()** closes the file to save the changes.

If **output.txt** doesn't exist, Python will create it. If it already exists, the content will be **overwritten**.

Step 2: Writing Multiple Lines to a File

If you want to write multiple lines to a file, you can use **write()** multiple times or write all the lines at once.

Example: Writing Multiple Lines

```
file = open("output.txt", "w")
file.write("First line\\n")
file.write("Second line\\n")
file.write("Third line\\n")
file.close()
```

Here, we are writing three lines to the file. Notice the **\\n** at the end of each line, which adds a **newline character** to move the cursor to the next line.

Alternatively, you can write all the lines at once by passing a list to the **writelines()** method:

```
lines = ["First line\\n", "Second line\\n", "Third line\\n"]
file = open("output.txt", "w")
file.writelines(lines)
file.close()
```

Step 3: Using the with Statement for Writing

Just like reading from a file, using the **with** statement is the best practice when writing to a file. It automatically closes the file when the writing process is done, even if an error occurs.

Example: Writing Using with

```
with open("output.txt", "w") as file:
    file.write("Hello, World!")
```

In this example:
- with open("output.txt", "w") as file opens the file in write mode.
- **file.write("Hello, World!")** writes the content to the file.
- The file is automatically closed when the block of code is finished, so you don't need to explicitly call **file.close()**.

Step 4: Appending Data to a File

If you want to **add** data to the end of an existing file without erasing its current contents, you can open the file in **append mode** by using **"a"**.

Example: Appending Data to a File

```
with open("output.txt", "a") as file:
  file.write("This is an additional line.\\n")
```

In this example:
- with open("output.txt", "a") as file opens the file in append mode.
- file.write("This is an additional line.\\\\n") adds a new line to the end of the file.

The original content of the file remains, and the new content is added at the end.

Step 5: Writing Data from Variables

You can also write data from variables to a file. For example, if you have a list or a number that you want to save to a file, you can convert it to a string and write it.

Example: Writing a List to a File

```
numbers = [1, 2, 3, 4, 5]

with open("numbers.txt", "w") as file:
  for number in numbers:
    file.write(f"{number}\\n")
```

Here, we:
Use a **for** loop to write each number in the list to the file, with each number on a new line.

Handling Large Files

If you are writing a lot of data to a file, you might want to break it down into smaller chunks or write line by line, especially if you are working with large datasets.

Example: Writing Large Data in Chunks

```
large_data = "A" * 1000000  # A string with 1 million characters

with open("large_file.txt", "w") as file:
    for i in range(0, len(large_data), 1000):  # Writing in chunks of 1000 characters
        file.write(large_data[i:i+1000])
```

In this example:
- We write large data to the file in **chunks** of 1000 characters at a time, instead of writing everything at once.

Fun Fact: Python Files Are Like Notebooks!
Think of a Python file as a notebook. When you open a file in write mode, it is like starting on a new page, and everything you write replaces what is there. When you open it in append mode, you are simply adding more notes to the end of your notebook!

Example: Saving the Results of a Quiz to a Text File

Let's build a simple **quiz** program where the user answers some questions, and at the end, their results (like score and answers) are saved to a text file. This example will demonstrate how to write data from a Python program into a file, allowing you to keep track of the quiz results.

Step 1: Creating the Quiz

First, we will write a basic quiz with a few questions. After each question, we will track whether the user's answer was correct or not and calculate the total score.

```
def run_quiz():
```

```
# List of questions and answers
questions = [
    {"question": "What is the capital of France?", "answer": "Paris"},
    {"question": "What is 5 + 7?", "answer": "12"},
    {"question": "Who wrote 'Harry Potter'?", "answer": "J.K. Rowling"}
]

# Variables to track the score and answers
score = 0
user_answers = []

# Loop through the questions
for q in questions:
    user_answer = input(q["question"] + " ")
    user_answers.append(user_answer)

    # Check if the answer is correct
    if user_answer.lower() == q["answer"].lower():
        print("Correct!")
        score += 1
    else:
        print(f"Wrong! The correct answer is {q['answer']}.")

return score, user_answers
```

In this example:
- We have three quiz questions stored in a list of dictionaries.
- The user inputs their answer for each question, and the program checks if the answer is correct.
- We keep track of the user's answers and the total score.

Step 2: Saving the Quiz Results to a File

After the quiz ends, we will save the user's score and their answers to a text file. This allows us to store the results for future reference.

Saving Results to a File:

```
def save_results(score, user_answers):
    with open("quiz_results.txt", "w") as file:
        file.write(f"Quiz Results\\n")
        file.write(f"Score: {score}/3\\n")
```

```
    file.write("Answers:\\n")

    for i, answer in enumerate(user_answers, 1):
        file.write(f"Question {i}: {answer}\\n")
```

In this function:
- We open the file **quiz_results.txt** in write mode.
- We write the user's score and their answers to the file.
- The **with** statement ensures the file is closed after writing.

Step 3: Running the Quiz and Saving the Results

Now we can combine the quiz and the result-saving function. After the user finishes the quiz, their results are saved automatically.

```
def main():
    print("Welcome to the Quiz!")

    # Run the quiz and get the score and answers
    score, user_answers = run_quiz()

    # Save the results to a file
    save_results(score, user_answers)

    print("Your results have been saved to quiz_results.txt!")

# Run the program
main()
```

In this **main()** function:
- We run the quiz using the **run_quiz()** function, which returns the user's score and answers.
- We then save the results to a file using the **save_results()** function.
- After saving, the program prints a message letting the user know their results have been saved.

Example Quiz Output

When the quiz is run, the user will answer the questions, and their score and answers will be saved to a file. Here is an example of what the **quiz_results.txt** file might look like:

quiz_results.txt:

Quiz Results
Score: 2/3
Answers:
Question 1: Paris
Question 2: 12
Question 3: J.K. Rowling

Step 4: Improving the Quiz

You can enhance the quiz by adding more questions, keeping track of incorrect answers, or allowing the user to play multiple rounds and store all the results in one file.

Example: Appending Results for Multiple Users:

```
def save_results(score, user_answers):
    with open("quiz_results.txt", "a") as file:  # Open in append mode
        file.write(f"\\nNew Quiz Attempt\\n")
        file.write(f"Score: {score}/3\\n")
        file.write("Answers:\\n")

        for i, answer in enumerate(user_answers, 1):
            file.write(f"Question {i}: {answer}\\n")
```

Now, each time the quiz is taken, the results will be added to the end of the file, keeping a record of all quiz attempts.

Fun Fact: Storing Quiz Results Is Like Keeping Scorecards!
Think of the quiz results file as a scorecard where you write down each player's performance. Every time you take the quiz, your results are saved, just like how players' scores are recorded after each game. The next time you take the quiz, you can look back at how you did before!

Fun Fact: Every Document, Image, and Video on Your Computer Is Stored in a File!

Did you know that everything you see on your computer—a word document, a family photo, or your favorite movie—is stored as a **file**? Files are like containers containing all the information for each document, image, or video. These files come in different formats, depending on the type of information they store.

What Is a File, Really?

A file is simply a collection of **data** stored on your computer. This data could be text, numbers, images, or even sound. When you open a file, your computer reads the data inside and presents it to you in a way that makes sense, whether it is a letter, a picture, or a video clip.

Types of Files

There are many different types of files, each designed for specific purposes:
- **Text Files**: These store written content like your notes, essays, or programming code. Examples include .txt, .docx, and .pdf files.
- **Image Files**: Photos and pictures are stored in files like .jpg, .png, and .gif.
- **Video Files**: Your favorite movies and YouTube videos are stored in formats like .mp4, .avi, and .mov.
- **Music Files**: Songs and sounds are stored in files like .mp3 and .wav.
Each type of file has its own format that tells your computer how to open and display the information inside.

How Do Files Work?

Behind the scenes, every file is just a collection of **binary data**—a series of 0s and 1s that computers can understand. For example, when you open a picture, your computer reads this binary data and turns it into pixels on your screen. When you watch a video, the computer plays the data in sequence to show you moving pictures and sound.

Your Computer Is Full of Files!

Every time you create something new on your computer, like a document or a picture, you are creating a file. Even the programs you use, like games and web browsers, are stored in files on your computer. That's why it is important to organize your files into folders and back them up regularly! Fun Fact: Even Your Apps Are Files!

Did you know that every app or program you use is made up of hundreds of files? From the code that runs the app to the icons and images that you see on the screen, all of these are stored in files. When you install an app, you are really just downloading a bunch of files that work together to make the app run smoothly!

Chapter 15: Handling Errors – Python the Detective

What Are Errors, and Why Do They Happen?

In programming, **errors** are mistakes or issues that prevent your code from running correctly. Like a detective solving a mystery, Python has to figure out what went wrong when encountering an error. Errors happen for many reasons, and understanding them is an important part of becoming a good programmer.

Why Do Errors Happen?

Errors can occur for several reasons. Sometimes, it is because of a typo in your code; other times, it is because the code is trying to do something impossible, like dividing a number by zero or trying to access a file that doesn't exist. Here are some common reasons why errors happen in Python:

Syntax Errors: These occur when the structure of your code does not follow the rules of Python's syntax. It's like writing a sentence without proper grammar.
- **Example**: Forgetting a colon at the end of a loop or a function definition.
- **Fix**: Make sure all Python syntax rules are followed, such as using colons, parentheses, and indentation correctly.

```
# Syntax error (missing colon)

for i in range(5)
    print(i)
```

Name Errors: These happen when you try to use a variable or function that hasn't been defined yet.
- **Example**: Using a variable age without creating it first.

- **Fix**: Ensure that all variables and functions are defined before using them.

```
# Name error (age is not defined)
print(age)
```

 Type Errors: These occur when you try to perform an operation on incompatible data types, like adding a string and a number.
- **Example**: Adding a string to an integer without converting the types.
- **Fix**: Convert data types when necessary or make sure you are using compatible types.

```
# Type error (cannot add string and integer)
name = "John"
age = 25
print(name + age)
```

Value Errors: These happen when you pass the wrong type of value to a function. For example, trying to convert the word "apple" into a number will cause a value error.
- **Example**: Using a string in a mathematical operation that expects a number.
- **Fix**: Check the values you are working with and ensure they match the function's expected input.

```
# Value error (cannot convert string to int)
number = int("apple")
```

ZeroDivisionError: This error occurs when your code tries to divide a number by zero, which is mathematically impossible.
- **Example**: Trying to calculate 10 / 0.
- **Fix**: Make sure the denominator in a division operation is not zero.

```
# ZeroDivisionError (division by zero is not allowed)
result = 10 / 0
```

File Errors: These occur when Python can't find or open a file you're trying to work with.
- **Example**: Trying to open a file that doesn't exist.
- **Fix**: Double-check the file path and ensure the file exists before attempting to open it.

```
# File error (file not found)
with open("non_existent_file.txt", "r") as file:
    content = file.read()
```

How Does Python Handle Errors?

When Python encounters an error, it immediately stops running the code and displays an **error message**. This message is called a **traceback**, and it provides useful information about what went wrong, including the type of error and the line of code where the error occurred. It's like a detective leaving clues for you to find and fix the problem!

For example, if you try to divide a number by zero, Python will raise a **ZeroDivisionError** and show you exactly where the issue occurred.

Common Types of Errors in Python

Here is a quick overview of some common errors you will encounter in Python:

Error Type	What It Means	Example
SyntaxError	You've broken Python's syntax rules.	Missing colons, parentheses, or indentation.
NameError	You're using a variable or function that hasn't been defined.	Referring to a variable before creating it.
TypeError	You're trying to perform an operation on incompatible types.	Adding a string to an integer.

ValueError	You've passed the wrong type of value to a function.	Converting non-numeric data to an integer.
ZeroDivisionError	You're trying to divide a number by zero.	Calculating 10 / 0.
FileNotFoundError	You're trying to access a file that doesn't exist.	Opening a file that doesn't exist.

Fun Fact: Programmers Make Mistakes Too!
Even the best programmers encounter errors in their code. Errors are a normal part of the coding process, and learning how to debug (find and fix errors) is an essential skill. Python's helpful error messages are like clues from a detective—they guide you to the exact spot in your code where something went wrong.

How to Handle Errors Using try and except

Errors are a normal part of programming, but they do not have to stop your program from running. In Python, you can use **try and except** blocks to handle errors gracefully. This way, when an error occurs, your program can **catch** it and continue running instead of crashing.

What Are try and except?

The **try** block is used to "try" running a piece of code that might cause an error. If an error occurs, instead of crashing the program, Python will jump to the **except** block, where you can handle the error in a safe way.

Syntax:

```
try:
    # Code that might cause an error
except:
    # Code to handle the error
```

Step 1: Using try and except to Catch Errors

Let's look at a simple example where we try to divide two numbers. Normally, dividing by zero would cause a **ZeroDivisionError** and crash the program. But with **try and except,** we can catch that error and handle it without crashing.

Example: Handling Division by Zero

```
try:
    result = 10 / 0
except ZeroDivisionError:
    print("Error: You can't divide by zero!")
```

In this example:
- **try:** contains the code that might cause an error (in this case, division by zero).
- If a **ZeroDivisionError** occurs, Python jumps to the **except ZeroDivisionError:** block and prints an error message instead of crashing the program.

Step 2: Handling Multiple Types of Errors

Sometimes, your code might raise different types of errors. You can catch and handle multiple error types by using multiple **except** blocks. Each block can handle a specific type of error.

Example: Handling Multiple Errors

```
try:
    number = int(input("Enter a number: "))
    result = 10 / number
except ZeroDivisionError:
    print("Error: You can't divide by zero!")
except ValueError:
    print("Error: Invalid input! Please enter a valid number.")
```

In this example:
- **ZeroDivisionError** is caught when the user tries to divide by zero.

- **ValueError** is caught when the user enters something that can't be converted to a number, like typing "apple" instead of a number.

Step 3: Catching All Errors with a General except Block

If you do not know what kind of error might occur, you can use a **general except block** to catch any error. This is useful when you want to make sure your program handles all possible errors, but it's often better to handle specific errors when possible.

Example: General Error Handling

```
try:
    result = 10 / int(input("Enter a number: "))
except Exception as e:
    print(f"An error occurred: {e}")
```

In this example:
- **except Exception as e:** catches any error and stores the error message in the variable **e**.
- The error message is then printed out, so you know what went wrong.

Step 4: Using else and finally

You can add two more optional blocks to your error-handling code:
- **else:** runs if no error occurs.
- **finally:** runs no matter what, whether an error happens or not. This is useful for closing files or cleaning up resources.

Example: Using else and finally

```
try:
    number = int(input("Enter a number: "))
    result = 10 / number
except ZeroDivisionError:
    print("Error: You can't divide by zero!")
except ValueError:
    print("Error: Invalid input! Please enter a valid number.")
else:
    print(f"Success! The result is {result}")
```

```
finally:
    print("This will always run, no matter what.")
```

In this example:
- The **else** block runs only if no errors occur.
- The **finally** block runs every time, whether there's an error or not. It's often used to clean up resources, like closing a file after reading or writing to it.

When Should You Use try and except?

You should use **try and except** when:
1. **You expect something might go wrong**: For example, when working with user input, reading files, or making network requests.
2. **You want to handle errors without stopping the program**: This is useful in applications that need to keep running, even if small issues occur.
3. **You want to provide helpful error messages**: Instead of letting your program crash, you can explain what went wrong to the user.

Fun Fact: Python Is Like a Safety Net!
Think of try and except as a safety net for your program. Just like a trapeze artist uses a net to catch them if they fall, Python uses try and except to catch errors and prevent your program from crashing. It's a great way to keep your code safe and running smoothly, even when something unexpected happens!

Example: Writing a Program That Keeps Working

Even When Something Goes Wrong

Let's write a program that runs smoothly even when errors occur. In this example, we will create a simple number-guessing game in which the user guesses a random number. We will add **error handling** to ensure the program does not crash if the user enters something invalid, like text instead of a number.

Step 1: Setting Up the Game

We will start by creating a basic number guessing game. The program will randomly select a number between 1 and 10, and the user will try to guess it. We will use Python's random library to generate the number.

Code: Basic Guessing Game

```python
import random

def guessing_game():
    secret_number = random.randint(1, 10)
    attempts = 0

    print("Welcome to the Number Guessing Game!")
    print("I have selected a number between 1 and 10.")

    while True:
        try:
            guess = int(input("Enter your guess: "))
            attempts += 1

            if guess < secret_number:
                print("Too low! Try again.")
            elif guess > secret_number:
                print("Too high! Try again.")
            else:
                print(f"Congratulations! You guessed the number in {attempts} attempts.")
                break
        except ValueError:
            print("Error: Please enter a valid number.")
```

Step 2: Handling Errors with try and except

In the guessing game:
- We use a **try block** to handle user input, specifically when the user enters their guess.
- If the user types something that can't be converted to an integer (like a word or special character), a **ValueError** will occur. This error is caught by the **except ValueError** block, which prints an error message and prompts the user to try again.

How It Works:
1. The program generates a random number between 1 and 10.
2. The user is prompted to guess the number.
3. If the user enters something that's not a valid number (like "apple" or "abc"), the **ValueError** is caught, and the program prints **"Error: Please enter a valid number."**
4. If the guess is too low or too high, the program gives feedback and continues to run until the correct number is guessed.

Step 3: Ensuring the Program Keeps Running

By using **try and except**, the program keeps running smoothly even when an error occurs. Without this error handling, the program would crash the moment the user entered an invalid input. Now, the user can keep guessing until they get it right, and the game won't stop unexpectedly.

Step 4: Example Run

Here is what a sample run of the game might look like:

Sample Output:

```
Welcome to the Number Guessing Game!
I have selected a number between 1 and 10.
Enter your guess: apple
Error: Please enter a valid number.
Enter your guess: 5
Too low! Try again.
Enter your guess: 8
Too high! Try again.
Enter your guess: 7
Congratulations! You guessed the number in 3 attempts.
```

In this example:
• The user initially enters "apple," which is not a valid number. The **ValueError** is caught, and the program prompts the user to enter a valid number.
• The user then guesses a series of numbers until they guess the correct one, and the game ends successfully.

Step 5: Adding More Features

To enhance the program, we can add additional error handling and features. For example, we could:

- **Limit the number of attempts**: If the user exceeds a certain number of guesses, the game could end.
- **Allow the user to quit**: The user could type "quit" to exit the game early, and we can handle this gracefully.

Code: Adding More Feature

```python
import random

def guessing_game():
    secret_number = random.randint(1, 10)
    attempts = 0
    max_attempts = 5

    print("Welcome to the Number Guessing Game!")
    print("I have selected a number between 1 and 10. Type 'quit' to exit the game.")

    while attempts < max_attempts:
        try:
            user_input = input("Enter your guess: ")

            if user_input.lower() == "quit":
                print("Thanks for playing! Goodbye.")
                break

            guess = int(user_input)
            attempts += 1

            if guess < secret_number:
                print("Too low! Try again.")
            elif guess > secret_number:
                print("Too high! Try again.")
            else:
                print(f"Congratulations! You guessed the number in {attempts} attempts.")
                break
        except ValueError:
            print("Error: Please enter a valid number.")

    if attempts == max_attempts:
```

```
    print(f"Sorry, you've reached the maximum number of attempts. The number
was {secret_number}.")
```

Step 6: Features Added

1. **Maximum Attempts**: We've added a limit of 5 attempts. If the user doesn't guess the correct number in 5 tries, the game ends.
2. **Quit Option**: The user can now type **"quit"** to exit the game early.
3. **Error Handling**: The **try and except** blocks ensure that invalid input (like words or symbols) doesn't crash the game.

Fun Fact: Error Handling Makes Programs More User-Friendly!
When users interact with programs, they don't always follow the expected rules. Error handling makes your programs more user-friendly by allowing them to recover from mistakes. It helps create a better experience by guiding users to the right input without abruptly stopping the program.

Fun Fact: Python Doesn't Get Angry When It Finds an Error – It Helps You Fix It!

Unlike humans, Python does not get frustrated when something goes wrong in your code. Instead, it **helps you figure out what is wrong** and gives you clues to fix the problem. When Python finds an error, it does not crash your computer or give up on your program. Instead, it prints an **error message** (a **traceback**) explaining what went wrong and where the mistake happened.

How Does Python Help You Fix Errors?

When Python encounters an error, it shows you:
- **The type of error**: For example, **SyntaxError**, **TypeError**, or **NameError**. Each error type has a specific meaning and points to what went wrong.
- **The line number**: Python tells you exactly which line in your code caused the error, making it easy to find and fix the problem.
- **A helpful message**: It provides a short explanation of the error. For example, if you forget to close a parenthesis, Python will say something like **"SyntaxError: unexpected EOF while parsing"**, letting you know there is an issue with your syntax.

181

Python gives you all the information you need to solve the problem—like a friendly coach who points out your mistakes and encourages you to try again.

Example: A Helpful Error Message

Let's say you write a program to divide two numbers, but you accidentally try to divide by zero:

```
result = 10 / 0
```

When you run the code, Python will display this error message:

```
ZeroDivisionError: division by zero
```

This message tells you exactly what went wrong: you tried to divide by zero, which is not allowed. Python isn't upset—it is just letting you know what to fix!

Traceback: Python's Detective Work

When an error happens, Python provides a **traceback**, which is like a detective's notebook. The traceback lists all the steps Python took before it found the error. It tells you:

- **The file** where the error occurred.
- **The line number** where the error happened.
- **The type of error** and a description of the problem.

This makes it easy to **track down the issue** and correct your code.

Fun Fact: Python Is Like a Teacher!
Think of Python as your coding teacher. When you make a mistake, it does not scold you or crash your program—it shows you what went wrong and helps you learn from the error. Every mistake is a learning opportunity, and Python is always there to guide you with clear, helpful messages!

Chapter 16: Building a Simple Game

Bringing It All Together: Writing Your First Text-Based Game

Now that you have learned the basics of Python, it is time to combine everything by creating your own **text-based game**! This project will combine many skills you have practiced, such as using variables, if statements, loops, functions, and handling errors. A text-based game is a great way to apply what you know and have fun while coding.

For this game, we will build a simple **adventure game** where the player explores a forest, faces challenges, and makes decisions that affect the outcome. It will be entirely text-based, meaning the player interacts with the game through text input, and the game responds with text descriptions and options.

Step 1: Planning the Game

Before we start coding, let's plan out the game. Here's a basic structure for our text-based adventure:

1. **Setting**: The player starts in a mysterious forest.
2. **Goal**: The player's goal is to find a hidden treasure while avoiding dangers like wild animals or getting lost.
3. **Choices**: At each stage of the game, the player will be presented with choices, and their decisions will affect what happens next.
4. **Challenges**: The player will encounter challenges (like fighting a wild animal or solving a riddle), and the game will use if statements to determine whether the player succeeds or fails.

Step 2: Setting Up the Game

Let's start by welcoming the player and setting the stage for the adventure.

```
def start_game():
    print("Welcome to the Adventure Game!")
    print("You find yourself in a mysterious forest, surrounded by tall trees and thick fog.")
    print("Your goal is to find the hidden treasure. But beware, danger lurks in the shadows!")
```

```
player_name = input("What is your name, brave adventurer? ")
print(f"Hello, {player_name}! Your adventure begins now...")

# Call the first part of the game
forest_path(player_name)
```

In this code:
- We welcome the player to the game and provide a brief description of the setting.
- The player enters their name, which will be used throughout the game to make the experience more personal.

Step 3: Creating the First Challenge

Now that the game has started, we will create the first challenge. The player must choose which path to take in the forest.

Code: Choosing a Path

```
def forest_path(player_name):
    print("\\nYou stand at a fork in the path.")
    print("To the left, you hear the sound of rushing water.")
    print("To the right, the path seems darker, but you sense a strange glow in the
distance.")

    choice = input("Which way will you go? Type 'left' or 'right': ").lower()

    if choice == "left":
        river_challenge(player_name)
    elif choice == "right":
        glowing_path_challenge(player_name)
    else:
        print("That's not a valid option. Try again.")
        forest_path(player_name)  # Restart the choice if input is invalid
```

In this section:
- The player is presented with a choice between two paths: left (toward the sound of water) or right (toward the strange glow).

184

- We use an **if-elif-else** structure to handle the player's choice and move them to the next part of the game based on their decision.

Step 4: Adding a Challenge

Let's create the challenge for the **left path**. The player encounters a fast-moving river and must figure out how to cross it

Code: River Challenge

```
def river_challenge(player_name):
    print("\\nYou arrive at the riverbank. The water is moving swiftly, and it's too deep
to wade through.")
    print("You notice a fallen tree that could be used as a bridge, but it looks unstable.")

    choice = input("What will you do? Type 'cross' to use the tree or 'turn back' to go
the other way: ").lower()

    if choice == "cross":
        print("You carefully step onto the tree...")
        success = random.randint(1, 2)  # Randomly determine if the player succeeds

        if success == 1:
            print(f"Congratulations, {player_name}! You crossed the river safely.")
            treasure_hunt(player_name)  # Move to the next part of the game
        else:
            print(f"Uh oh! The tree snaps, and you fall into the river. Game over,
{player_name}.")
    elif choice == "turn back":
        print(f"{player_name}, you decide it's too dangerous and head back to the fork in
the path.")
        forest_path(player_name)  # Send the player back to the path
    else:
        print("That's not a valid option. Try again.")
        river_challenge(player_name)  # Restart the challenge if input is invalid
```

In this challenge:
- The player must choose whether to **cross the river** using a fallen tree or **turn back.**
- If the player chooses to cross the river, the outcome is determined randomly using random.randint(), making the game more exciting.

185

- If the player fails to cross the river, the game ends. If they succeed, the adventure continues.

Step 5: Adding Another Challenge

Now let's create a challenge for the **right path**. The player encounters a strange glowing object and must decide whether to investigate.

Code: Glowing Path Challenge

```
def glowing_path_challenge(player_name):
    print("\\nYou follow the glowing path and soon come upon a glowing crystal lying on the ground.")
    print("It hums with energy, and the air around it feels charged with electricity.")

    choice = input("Will you pick up the crystal? Type 'yes' or 'no': ").lower()

    if choice == "yes":
        print(f"As you touch the crystal, {player_name}, you feel a surge of power!")
        print("You gain the strength to overcome any challenge. The treasure must be close!")
        treasure_hunt(player_name)  # Move to the treasure hunt
    elif choice == "no":
        print("You decide it's best not to disturb the mysterious crystal and head back to the fork in the path.")
        forest_path(player_name)  # Return to the fork in the path
    else:
        print("That's not a valid option. Try again.")
        glowing_path_challenge(player_name)  # Restart the challenge if input is invalid
```

In this challenge:
- The player encounters a glowing crystal and must decide whether to **pick it up** or **leave it**.
- Picking up the crystal gives the player extra strength to face the next challenge.

Step 6: The Final Challenge – The Treasure Hunt

Now, let's wrap up the game with the final challenge: finding the hidden treasure.

Code: The Treasure Hunt

```
def treasure_hunt(player_name):
    print("\\nYou reach a clearing in the forest, and in the center, you see an old chest
buried in the ground.")
    print("But there's one last challenge! A riddle is carved into the chest:")
    print("'I speak without a mouth and hear without ears. I have no body, but I come
alive with the wind. What am I?'")

    answer = input("What is your answer? ").lower()

    if answer == "echo":
        print(f"Congratulations, {player_name}! You solved the riddle and found the
hidden treasure!")
        print("You open the chest and claim your reward. Victory is yours!")
    else:
        print("That's not the correct answer. The chest remains locked, and your
adventure ends here.")
```

In this final challenge:
- The player must solve a riddle to unlock the treasure chest.
- If the player answers correctly (the answer is "echo"), they win the game and claim the treasure.

Fun Fact: Text-Based Games Were the First Computer Games!
Before we had amazing graphics and realistic video games, all games were text-based. Players would interact with the game by typing commands, and the game would respond with descriptions of what happened next. These early games sparked the imagination and are still fun to play and create today!

Example: A Simple Adventure Game Where the Player Makes Choices and Sees the Result

In this section, we will build a **simple text-based adventure game** that allows players to make choices and see the results of their decisions. This game will take everything you've learned so far—like using variables, if statements, loops, and functions—and combine them into a fun, interactive experience.

In this adventure game, the player explores a mysterious forest, faces challenges, and makes choices that affect the outcome. The player can take multiple paths, each leading to a different result.

Step 1: Setting Up the Game

We will start by welcoming the player, introducing the setting, and asking them for their name. This makes the game more engaging and personal.

Code: Game Introduction

```
def start_game():
    print("Welcome to the Forest Adventure!")
    print("You find yourself at the edge of a dense, mysterious forest. The sun is setting,
and you must decide how to proceed.")
    player_name = input("What is your name, brave adventurer? ")
    print(f"Hello, {player_name}! Your journey begins now...")

    # Call the first part of the game
    forest_path(player_name)
```

In this code:
- The game starts by giving the player a brief description of the setting.
- The player enters their name, which we will use throughout the game.
- After the introduction, the game calls the **forest_path()** function, where the first challenge begins.

Step 2: The First Choice – Left or Right?

In this part of the game, the player stands at a fork in the path and must decide whether to go left or right. Each choice will lead to a different challenge.

Code: The Fork in the Path

```
def forest_path(player_name):
    print("\\nYou stand at a fork in the path.")
    print("To your left, you hear the sound of a waterfall. To your right, the path leads
deeper into the forest, where the trees are thick and the air is still.")

    choice = input("Which way will you go? Type 'left' or 'right': ").lower()
```

```
if choice == "left":
    waterfall_challenge(player_name)
elif choice == "right":
    forest_challenge(player_name)
else:
    print("That's not a valid option. Try again.")
    forest_path(player_name)  # Restart if invalid input
```

In this section:
- The player is presented with two options: **left** (toward the waterfall) or **right** (deeper into the forest).
- Based on their choice, the game will call either the **waterfall_challenge()** or **forest_challenge()** function, which leads to a different adventure.

Step 3: The Waterfall Challenge

If the player chooses to go left, they will encounter a waterfall and must make a choice about how to proceed.

Code: Waterfall Challenge

```
def waterfall_challenge(player_name):
    print("\\nYou follow the path to the left and soon arrive at a beautiful waterfall.")
    print("The water rushes over the rocks, and you see something shiny at the base of
the waterfall.")

    choice = input("Will you wade through the water to investigate, or stay on the dry
path? Type 'investigate' or 'stay': ").lower()

    if choice == "investigate":
        print(f"You wade through the water, {player_name}, and discover a hidden
treasure chest!")
        print(f"Congratulations, {player_name}! You've found the treasure!")
    elif choice == "stay":
        print(f"You decide to stay dry and continue down the path, {player_name}.")
        print("After a long walk, you find yourself back at the starting point, but with no
treasure.")
    else:
        print("That's not a valid option. Try again.")
        waterfall_challenge(player_name)
```

In this part:
- The player arrives at a waterfall and must choose to either **investigate** the shiny object or **stay** on the dry path.
- If they investigate, they find a treasure chest and win the game. If they stay on the path, they miss out on the treasure.

Step 4: The Forest Challenge

If the player chooses to go right, they will encounter a dark forest with a mysterious creature. They must decide how to react.

Code: Forest Challenge

```
def forest_challenge(player_name):
    print("\\nYou take the path to the right, and the trees grow thicker and the air colder.")
    print("Suddenly, you hear rustling in the bushes, and a large wolf steps into the path.")

    choice = input("Will you try to run or stand your ground? Type 'run' or 'stand': ").lower()

    if choice == "run":
        print(f"You turn and run as fast as you can, {player_name}!")
        print("You manage to escape, but you're now lost in the forest.")
    elif choice == "stand":
        print(f"You stand your ground, {player_name}, and the wolf slowly backs away, leaving you unharmed.")
        print("With newfound courage, you continue your journey and find a hidden cave full of treasure!")
    else:
        print("That's not a valid option. Try again.")
        forest_challenge(player_name)
```

In this part:
- The player encounters a wolf and must decide to either **run** or **stand their ground**.
- Running leads to getting lost, while standing their ground results in finding treasure.

Step 5: Wrapping Up the Game

Once the player has faced a challenge, the game either ends with success or they can start over by returning to the beginning.

Code: Game Over

```
def game_over(player_name, success):
    if success:
        print(f"Congratulations, {player_name}! You've successfully completed the
adventure!")
    else:
        print(f"Sorry, {player_name}, your adventure has come to an end.")

    replay = input("Would you like to play again? Type 'yes' or 'no': ").lower()
    if replay == "yes":
        start_game()
    else:
        print("Thanks for playing!")
```

In this part:
- If the player succeeds, they are congratulated. If not, the game offers them the chance to play again.
- The player can choose to replay the game, which restarts the adventure.

Fun Fact: Text-Based Games Are All About Imagination!
Before video games had amazing graphics, people played text-based games where they had to imagine the entire world. These games were all about making choices, exploring virtual worlds, and facing challenges, just like the game we've built here!

Adding Loops, If Statements, and Variables to Make the Game Interactive

To make your adventure game more interactive, we can use Python features like **loops**, **if statements**, and **variables**. These features allow the player to make choices, face challenges, and experience different outcomes based on their decisions. In this section, we'll focus on using these tools to enhance the game's interactivity, making it more dynamic and engaging.

191

Step 1: Using Loops to Keep the Game Running

One of the best ways to keep your game interactive is by using **loops**. Loops allow the game to continue running until the player reaches an ending (such as finding treasure or getting lost). We can use a **while loop** to repeat sections of the game until the player makes a decision or encounters an ending.

Example: Using a Loop for Game Flow

```python
def start_game():
    print("Welcome to the Forest Adventure!")

    while True:
        player_name = input("What is your name, brave adventurer? ")
        if player_name:
            break  # Exit the loop once a valid name is entered
        else:
            print("Please enter a valid name.")

    print(f"Hello, {player_name}! Your adventure begins now...")
    forest_path(player_name)
```

In this example:
- We use a **while loop** to keep asking for the player's name until they enter a valid one.
- The game only proceeds to the adventure once the player provides a name.

Step 2: Using If Statements for Decision-Making

If statements allow the game to react to the player's decisions. When the player is presented with choices (like going left or right), if statements help the game decide what happens next based on their input.

Example: Making Decisions with If Statements

```python
def forest_path(player_name):
    print("\\nYou stand at a fork in the path.")
    print("To the left, you hear the sound of rushing water.")
```

```
    print("To the right, the path leads deeper into the forest.")

    choice = input("Which way will you go? Type 'left' or 'right': ").lower()

    if choice == "left":
        print(f"You head toward the sound of water, {player_name}.")
        waterfall_challenge(player_name)
    elif choice == "right":
        print(f"You venture deeper into the forest, {player_name}.")
        forest_challenge(player_name)
    else:
        print("That's not a valid option. Try again.")
        forest_path(player_name)  # Ask again if the input is invalid
```

In this part:

- We use **if-elif-else** statements to determine which path the player takes based on their input.
- If the player makes an invalid choice, the game asks them to try again by calling the function recursively.

Step 3: Using Variables to Track Player Choices

Variables help track important information about the player's progress or actions. For example, you can use variables to keep track of the player's **health, score,** or **inventory.**

Example: Tracking Health Points

Let's add a **health** variable to make the game more interactive. The player will lose health points if they make risky decisions.

```
def start_game():
    player_name = input("What is your name, brave adventurer? ")
    health = 3  # Starting health points

    print(f"Hello, {player_name}! You have {health} health points.")
    forest_path(player_name, health)

def forest_path(player_name, health):
    print("\\nYou stand at a fork in the path.")
    choice = input("Which way will you go? Type 'left' or 'right': ").lower()
```

```
    if choice == "left":
        health = waterfall_challenge(player_name, health)
    elif choice == "right":
        health = forest_challenge(player_name, health)
    else:
        print("Invalid option. Try again.")
        forest_path(player_name, health)

    # Check if the player is out of health
    if health <= 0:
        print(f"Sorry, {player_name}, you have run out of health. Game over!")
    else:
        print(f"{player_name}, you have {health} health points left. Choose your next
path.")
        forest_path(player_name, health)  # Continue the adventure
```

How It Works:
- The **health** variable tracks the player's health points. The player starts
  with 3 health points.
- Each time the player makes a risky choice, their health might decrease.
- If the player's health reaches zero, the game ends.

Step 4: Adding Challenges That Affect Variables

Now let's create a challenge where the player's health is affected based on
their decisions. If the player makes a risky decision, they'll lose a health
point.

Example: River Challenge with Health Points

```
def waterfall_challenge(player_name, health):
    print("\\nYou arrive at the riverbank.")
    print("The water is moving fast, and you notice a fallen tree that could be used as a
bridge.")

    choice = input("Do you want to cross the river? Type 'yes' or 'no': ").lower()

    if choice == "yes":
        print(f"You attempt to cross the river, {player_name}.")
        success = random.randint(1, 2)  # Randomly determine success
```

```
    if success == 1:
        print("You crossed the river safely!")
    else:
        print(f"The tree snaps! You fall into the water and lose 1 health point,
{player_name}.")
        health -= 1  # Decrease health by 1
  elif choice == "no":
    print(f"You decide not to risk it, {player_name}.")
  else:
    print("Invalid option. Try again.")
    return waterfall_challenge(player_name, health)  # Retry the challenge

  return health  # Return the updated health
```

In this example:
- If the player chooses to cross the river, the outcome is determined randomly using random.randint().
- If they fail, they lose a health point.
- The **health** variable is updated after the challenge and returned to the main game flow.

Step 5: Making the Game Replayable

To make the game more fun, we can add a **loop** that allows the player to keep playing even after they finish the game. This way, they can try different paths and see different outcomes.

Example: Replay Option

```
def game_over(player_name, health):
    if health > 0:
        print(f"Congratulations, {player_name}, you survived the adventure with {health}
health points!")
    else:
        print(f"Sorry, {player_name}, you ran out of health. Game over!")

    replay = input("Would you like to play again? Type 'yes' or 'no': ").lower()
    if replay == "yes":
        start_game()
    else:
        print("Thanks for playing!")
```

In this part:
- After the game ends, the player is given the option to replay.
- If they choose **yes**, the game restarts from the beginning.

Fun Fact: Loops Keep Games Running Smoothly!
Many of your favorite video games use loops to keep things running smoothly.
Whether it's a loop checking for player input or a loop that keeps the game world
moving, loops are essential for making games interactive and dynamic!

Fun Fact: Many Famous Games, Like Minecraft, Started with Simple Code Just Like This!

Did you know that some of the most famous video games in the world
started out with **simple code**? Games like **Minecraft**, which millions of
people play today, began as small projects written by individual
programmers. Minecraft's creator, Markus Persson (also known as Notch),
started by writing a simple game where players could place and destroy
blocks in a virtual world. Over time, this small project grew into one of the
most successful games ever!

How Do Big Games Start Small?

Most big games don't start with complex graphics or detailed worlds. They
often begin with simple ideas, like:
- Moving a character across the screen.
- Jumping over obstacles.
- Collecting items or solving puzzles.

These basic ideas are then built upon, adding more features, challenges,
and improvements. The key to building a great game is to start small, like
the **text-based adventure** you're creating, and then keep improving it as
you learn more about programming.

Minecraft: From Blocks to a Global Phenomenon

Minecraft, one of the world's best-selling games, started out with very
simple gameplay. It allowed players to:
- Place blocks to build structures.
- Destroy blocks to gather resources.

Over time, more features were added, like:

- Survival mode, where players have to gather food and defend against enemies.
- Creative mode, where players can build anything they can imagine without limits.

What began as a simple block-placing game grew into a game that allows players to build entire cities, fight monsters, explore new worlds, and play with friends online. But at its core, Minecraft's success comes from simple code and basic mechanics—just like the code you're writing in your adventure game!

How Can You Turn Simple Code Into Something Bigger?

Like Minecraft, your game can grow as you add new ideas. Start with simple things, like making choices and exploring, then build on that by:

- Adding new challenges and paths for the player to explore.
- Creating different endings based on the choices the player makes.
- Introducing new features like inventory systems where the player can collect items.

The more you experiment with Python, the more creative you can be in expanding your game!

Fun Fact: Coding Is Like Building With Blocks!
Programming a game is like building with blocks. Each piece of code you write is like placing a block in Minecraft—it may seem simple at first, but when you put enough pieces together, you can create something amazing. The best part? You can always go back and change or improve what you've built, just like you can with a Minecraft structure.

198

Chapter 17: Exploring What You Can Do with Python

Python for Web Development (Django, Flask)

Did you know that Python is not just for games or small scripts? It is also a powerful tool for **web development**! Many websites and web applications are built using Python, thanks to two popular web frameworks: **Django** and **Flask**. These frameworks make it easier to create websites, web apps, and online tools with Python.

What Is Web Development?

Web development is the process of building websites and web applications that run on the internet. There are two parts to web development:

1. **Frontend**: What the user sees, like the design, buttons, and images on a website.
2. **Backend**: The part of the website that works behind the scenes. It handles things like saving data, managing user accounts, and making sure everything runs smoothly. This is where Python comes in!

Python is mainly used for the **backend** of web development, where it helps with tasks like:

- **Handling user data** (like signing in and saving preferences).
- Storing and retrieving information from a database.
- **Generating web pages** based on user input.

Django – The All-In-One Web Framework

Django is one of the most popular Python web frameworks, and it's known for being **"batteries-included"**. This means it comes with a lot of built-in tools and features that make web development faster and easier.

Why Use Django?

- **Everything is included**: Django has all the tools you need to build a website, like user authentication (logging in and out), managing a database, and even an admin panel for managing your site.
- **Faster development**: With Django, you don't have to build everything from scratch. It has built-in functions for common tasks, so you can focus on the unique parts of your site.
- **Security**: Django is designed to help you avoid common security mistakes, like exposing sensitive user data.

What Can You Build with Django?

- **Blogs**: Create a website where users can write, edit, and post blog articles.
- **E-commerce sites**: Build an online store with products, shopping carts, and checkout systems.
- **Social networks**: Create your own platform where users can connect, share posts, and send messages.

Example: Creating a Simple Blog with Django

In Django, you can create a blog by setting up models for blog posts, views to display the posts, and templates to create the HTML pages.

Here's a simple example of what a **model** for a blog post looks like in Django:

```
from django.db import models

class BlogPost(models.Model):
    title = models.CharField(max_length=100)
    content = models.TextField()
    date_posted = models.DateTimeField(auto_now_add=True)

    def __str__(self):
        return self.title
```

In this code:

- **BlogPost** is a class representing each blog post, with fields like **title**, **content**, and **date_posted**.
- This information will be saved in a **database** and displayed on the website when users visit the blog.

Flask – The Lightweight Framework

If Django is like a complete toolkit, **Flask** is like a blank canvas. It is a **lightweight** web framework that gives you more control and flexibility, but it does not come with as many built-in tools as Django. This makes Flask a great choice for **smaller projects** or developers who want to customize everything themselves.

Why Use Flask?

- **Minimalistic**: Flask gives you the freedom to build your app the way you want, without any unnecessary features.
- **Flexibility**: Because Flask is lightweight, you can easily add the features you need, one at a time.
- **Great for learning**: If you're just getting started with web development, Flask is easy to pick up because of its simplicity.

What Can You Build with Flask?

- **Simple web apps**: Create basic websites or web apps, like personal portfolios or small interactive tools.
- **APIs**: Flask is great for building **APIs** (interfaces that let other programs communicate with your app).
- **Prototypes**: If you want to quickly test an idea for a web app, Flask allows you to get a working version up and running fast.

Example: Creating a Simple Web Page with Flask

Here is an example of how easy it is to create a simple web page using Flask:

```
from flask import Flask

app = Flask(__name__)

@app.route('/')
def home():
```

201

```
    return "Hello, World! Welcome to my website."

if __name__ == '__main__':
    app.run(debug=True)
```

In this code:
- **Flask** is used to create a small web server.
- The **@app.route('/')** decorator tells Flask that the function **home()** should run when the user visits the homepage (/).
- The **app.run()** command starts the web server and makes your app accessible in the browser.

Django vs. Flask: Which One Should You Use?

Django	Flask
All-in-one, batteries-included	Lightweight and flexible
Great for large, complex projects	Great for small, simple projects
Lots of built-in features like authentication and database management	Minimal setup, allows you to add only what you need
Best for full-fledged websites	Best for prototypes, small apps, or APIs

Fun Fact: Many Popular Websites Are Built with Python!
Python is behind the scenes in many popular websites you use every day! Instagram, Pinterest, and YouTube all use Python to manage millions of users and deliver content to their platforms. Django and Flask make it possible to build powerful, scalable web apps using simple Python code!

Python for Data Science and Machine Learning

Python is one of the most popular languages for **data science** and **machine learning**, two fields that are transforming industries by using data to make predictions, uncover patterns, and solve complex problems. With powerful libraries and tools, Python helps data scientists and machine learning engineers analyze data, build models, and create intelligent applications.

What Is Data Science?

Data science involves analyzing large amounts of data to find patterns, make predictions, and gain insights. Companies use data science to understand customer behavior, improve products, and make better decisions. For example, **Netflix** uses data science to recommend shows you might like based on your viewing history, while **Amazon** uses it to suggest products you may want to buy.

Python is widely used in data science because it offers easy-to-use libraries that handle everything from data cleaning and visualization to advanced statistical analysis.

Popular Python Libraries for Data Science

1. **Pandas**: Used for data manipulation and analysis. Pandas makes it easy to work with large datasets and perform operations like filtering, grouping, and merging data.
2. **NumPy**: A fundamental package for scientific computing, NumPy supports arrays and matrices, along with a collection of mathematical functions to operate on them.
3. **Matplotlib**: A popular plotting library that allows you to create a wide range of visualizations, from basic line charts to complex histograms and 3D plots.
4. **Seaborn**: Built on top of Matplotlib, Seaborn is used for making statistical plots that are visually appealing and easy to interpret.
5. **Scikit-learn**: One of the most widely used machine learning libraries, Scikit-learn provides simple tools for building models, training algorithms, and making predictions.

What Is Machine Learning?

Machine learning is a branch of artificial intelligence (AI) that focuses on teaching computers to learn from data. Instead of being explicitly programmed to perform tasks, machine learning algorithms allow computers to **learn** from patterns in data and make decisions based on that knowledge.

For example:

- **Spam detection**: Machine learning algorithms analyze millions of emails to learn the patterns that distinguish spam from legitimate messages.

- **Self-driving cars**: Machine learning is used to teach cars how to recognize pedestrians, road signs, and other vehicles, allowing them to navigate safely.
- **Personalized recommendations**: Sites like **YouTube** and **Spotify** use machine learning to suggest videos and music based on your past preferences.

Popular Python Libraries for Machine Learning

1. **Scikit-learn**: A user-friendly library that provides tools for machine learning tasks like classification, regression, and clustering. It includes many pre-built algorithms for common tasks like predicting outcomes or categorizing data.
2. **TensorFlow**: A powerful library developed by Google, TensorFlow is used for building complex machine learning models, especially deep learning models with neural networks.
3. **Keras**: Built on top of TensorFlow, Keras provides a simple interface for creating and training neural networks, making it easier to experiment with deep learning models.
4. **PyTorch**: Another popular deep learning library, PyTorch is widely used in research for creating and training neural networks.
5. **XGBoost**: A machine learning library designed for speed and performance, often used for winning machine learning competitions and making predictions with large datasets.

Step-by-Step: A Simple Data Science Example

Let's walk through a simple data science project using Python. Imagine we have a dataset containing information about students' grades, and we want to analyze the data to find trends, like which students are performing well or which factors influence their grades.

Step 1: Importing Data with Pandas

We'll use **Pandas** to load and explore the dataset.

```
import pandas as pd

# Load the dataset
data = pd.read_csv('student_grades.csv')
```

```
# Display the first few rows of the dataset
print(data.head())
```

In this example:
Pandas is used to read the dataset from a CSV file and display the first few rows so we can understand its structure.

Step 2: Cleaning and Analyzing Data

Next, we will clean the data by removing any missing values and calculate basic statistics.

```
# Remove rows with missing values
data = data.dropna()

# Calculate the average grade
average_grade = data['Grade'].mean()
print(f"The average grade is: {average_grade}")
```

In this code:
- **Dropna()** is used to remove rows with missing values.
- We calculate the average grade to get a sense of how students are performing.

Step 3: Visualizing Data with Matplotlib

We will create a simple bar chart to visualize the number of students in each grade category.

```
import matplotlib.pyplot as plt

# Create a bar chart showing the number of students in each grade category
data['Grade'].value_counts().plot(kind='bar')
plt.title('Distribution of Student Grades')
plt.xlabel('Grade')
plt.ylabel('Number of Students')
plt.show()
```

This code creates a **bar chart** that shows the distribution of student grades, giving us a visual understanding of how students are performing.

Step-by-Step: A Simple Machine Learning Example

Let's now build a simple machine learning model using **Scikit-learn** to predict whether students will pass or fail based on their grades and study habits.

Step 1: Preparing the Data

We will prepare the data by selecting the features we want to use (like study hours and attendance) and the target (whether the student passed or failed).

```
from sklearn.model_selection import train_test_split

# Select features (e.g., study hours, attendance) and target (pass/fail)
features = data[['Study_Hours', 'Attendance']]
target = data['Pass_Fail']

# Split the data into training and testing sets
X_train, X_test, y_train, y_test = train_test_split(features, target, test_size=0.2,
random_state=42)
```

Step 2: Training a Machine Learning Model

We will use a **decision tree** algorithm to train the model on the training data.

```
from sklearn.tree import DecisionTreeClassifier

# Initialize the decision tree model
model = DecisionTreeClassifier()

# Train the model on the training data
model.fit(X_train, y_train)
```

Step 3: Making Predictions

Now that the model is trained, we can use it to make predictions on the test data.

```
# Make predictions on the test set
predictions = model.predict(X_test)

# Display the predictions
print(predictions)
```

Step 4: Evaluating the Model

Finally, we evaluate how well the model performed by comparing its predictions to the actual results.

```
from sklearn.metrics import accuracy_score

# Calculate the accuracy of the model
accuracy = accuracy_score(y_test, predictions)
print(f"The model's accuracy is: {accuracy * 100:.2f}%")
```

Fun Fact: Machine Learning Powers Your Everyday Life!
Machine learning is all around you, powering everything from your smartphone's voice assistant to the recommendations you see on Netflix. Every time you interact with these systems, you're using the power of machine learning to get personalized results!

Python for Automating Tasks (e.g., Organizing Files or Sending Emails)

One of the coolest things about Python is its ability to **automate repetitive tasks**, saving you time and effort. Whether you need to organize files, send emails, or scrape information from the web, Python can help you get the job done quickly and efficiently. With Python's wide range of libraries and modules, you can automate almost anything, turning boring tasks into something that happens at the click of a button.

What Is Task Automation?

Task automation refers to the process of using code to handle routine tasks that you would otherwise have to do manually. By writing Python scripts, you can:

- **Organize files** into folders based on their types (e.g., sorting documents, images, and videos).
- Rename files in bulk.
- **Send automated emails** to one or multiple recipients.
- **Scrape data** from websites to collect information automatically.
- **Backup files** or sync folders regularly.

Python makes task automation easy because it offers libraries and tools for interacting with files, emails, and even the web.

Automating File Organization

Imagine you have a folder full of documents, images, and videos all mixed together. It would take forever to sort them manually, but Python can do it in just a few lines of code.

Step 1: Organizing Files by Type

Let's write a Python script that automatically organizes files into different folders based on their type (e.g., .txt, .jpg, .mp4).

Code: Organizing Files

```
import os
import shutil

def organize_files(folder_path):
    # Define the folder names for each file type
    file_types = {
        'Documents': ['.pdf', '.docx', '.txt'],
        'Images': ['.jpg', '.png', '.jpeg'],
        'Videos': ['.mp4', '.avi'],
    }

    # Create the folders if they don't exist
    for folder in file_types.keys():
        os.makedirs(os.path.join(folder_path, folder), exist_ok=True)

    # Loop through all the files in the folder
```

```
    for filename in os.listdir(folder_path):
        file_path = os.path.join(folder_path, filename)

        # Skip directories
        if os.path.isdir(file_path):
            continue

        # Move files to the appropriate folder based on file extension
        file_extension = os.path.splitext(filename)[1]
        for folder, extensions in file_types.items():
            if file_extension in extensions:
                shutil.move(file_path, os.path.join(folder_path, folder, filename))
                break

# Provide the path to the folder you want to organize
folder_path = '/path/to/your/folder'
organize_files(folder_path)
```

In this script:
- We define **folders** for each file type, like Documents, Images, and Videos.
- The **os** module is used to create folders and interact with files.
- The **shutil** module is used to **move files** into the appropriate folders based on their extensions.
- The script automatically organizes the files, sorting them into their respective folders.

Automating Email Sending

Another common task you can automate is **sending emails**. Whether it is sending daily reports, notifications, or reminders, Python can do it all without you lifting a finger.

Step 2: Sending Automated Emails
We will use Python's built-in **smtplib** library to send an email automatically. You can customize the email content and send it to multiple recipients.

Code: Sending an Email

```
import smtplib
```

```
from email.mime.text import MIMEText

def send_email(sender_email, recipient_email, subject, body):
    # Create the email content
    message = MIMEText(body)
    message['From'] = sender_email
    message['To'] = recipient_email
    message['Subject'] = subject

    # Connect to the SMTP server (example using Gmail)
    with smtplib.SMTP_SSL('smtp.gmail.com', 465) as server:
        server.login(sender_email, 'your_password')
        server.sendmail(sender_email, recipient_email, message.as_string())

# Example usage
send_email(
    sender_email='your_email@gmail.com',
    recipient_email='recipient@example.com',
    subject='Automated Email',
    body='This is an automatically generated email sent by Python!'
)
```

In this script:
- We use **smtplib** to connect to Gmail's SMTP server.
- The **MIMEText** class formats the email body, including the subject and recipient.
- The **send_email()** function takes the sender's email, recipient's email, subject, and body as parameters, and sends the email automatically.

Automating Web Scraping

You can also use Python to **scrape data** from websites. This is useful when you want to gather information, like prices from e-commerce sites, news articles, or weather updates, automatically.

Step 3: Scraping Data from the Web

We will use the **BeautifulSoup** library to extract information from a web page.

Code: Scraping a Web Page

```
import requests
```

```
from bs4 import BeautifulSoup

def scrape_weather():
    # URL of the weather page to scrape
    url = '<https://example.com/weather>'

    # Get the web page content
    response = requests.get(url)
    soup = BeautifulSoup(response.text, 'html.parser')

    # Extract the weather information
    weather = soup.find('div', class_='weather-info').get_text()

    print(f"Today's weather: {weather}")

# Run the scraping function
scrape_weather()
```

In this script:
- **requests** is used to fetch the web page content.
- **BeautifulSoup** parses the HTML and extracts specific information, like the weather forecast.
- This simple script automatically retrieves data from the web, making it a powerful tool for data collection.

Automating Repetitive Tasks with Scheduling

You can take automation even further by scheduling tasks to run automatically at specific times or intervals. For example, you can set Python to **organize files every day** or **send an email reminder** every week.

Step 4: Scheduling Tasks

The **schedule** library allows you to easily schedule your Python scripts.

Code: Scheduling a Task

```
import schedule
import time
```

```
def send_reminder():
    print("This is your automated reminder!")

# Schedule the reminder to run every day at 10:00 AM
schedule.every().day.at("10:00").do(send_reminder)

# Keep the script running
while True:
    schedule.run_pending()
    time.sleep(1)
```

In this example:
- The script uses the **schedule** library to run the **send_reminder()** function every day at 10:00 AM.
- The **while loop** keeps the program running, constantly checking for scheduled tasks.

Fun Fact: Automation Saves You Time and Effort!
Automation is like having a personal assistant who takes care of boring or repetitive tasks for you. Imagine having Python automatically organize your files or send out email reminders while you focus on more important things. Once you set up an automation script, it keeps working for you without any extra effort!

Fun Fact: Python Is Used by Companies Like Google, NASA, and Pixar!

Python might seem like a simple programming language, but it is one of the most widely used tools in the world—and not just by hobbyists or students. Some of the biggest and most innovative companies on the planet, including **Google**, **NASA**, and **Pixar**, use Python for a variety of powerful tasks.

Google Uses Python for Search and Machine Learning

When you search for something on **Google**, Python is working behind the scenes to help provide the best results. Python is one of the main languages used at Google, especially for handling tasks like:
- **Data analysis**: Google uses Python to process the massive amounts of data it collects to provide faster and more accurate search results.

- **Machine learning**: Google's machine learning tools, like **TensorFlow**, are often built with Python, allowing engineers to create powerful models that learn from data and improve over time.
- **Automation**: Python helps automate tasks like managing servers, running tests, and analyzing performance, making Google's systems more efficient.

NASA Uses Python for Space Exploration

Even **NASA** uses Python to explore the mysteries of space! Python is used in various NASA projects, including:

- **Data analysis**: NASA collects vast amounts of data from spacecraft, satellites, and telescopes. Python is used to analyze this data to understand space phenomena, track spacecraft, and make scientific discoveries.
- **Simulations**: Python helps simulate complex systems, such as spacecraft trajectories or the behavior of celestial objects. By running simulations, NASA can predict how spacecraft will behave in space and plan missions more accurately.
- **Robotics**: Python is also used in robotic systems that assist with space missions, such as the **Mars rovers**. These robots gather data and send it back to Earth, where Python is used to process and analyze the information.

Pixar Uses Python for Animation

You have probably seen some of Pixar's amazing animated movies like **Toy Story** and **Finding Nemo**, but did you know Python played a part in creating them? Pixar uses Python in several stages of their animation pipeline:

- **Scripting**: Python is used to write scripts that automate various parts of the animation process, from organizing assets to setting up scenes. This helps animators focus on the creative aspects of their work.
- **Rendering**: Python helps manage the complex rendering process, where 3D models and animations are turned into the final images you see on the screen. With Python, Pixar can automate tasks like rendering scenes or creating special effects.
- **Tool development**: Python is also used to create custom tools that help animators and artists. These tools make it easier to design

characters, create motion, and apply textures, speeding up the animation process.

Why Do These Companies Love Python?

Python's popularity in companies like Google, NASA, and Pixar comes from its **simplicity**, **versatility**, and **power**. Here are a few reasons why Python is their go-to language:

- Easy to learn: Python's straightforward syntax makes it easy for engineers, data scientists, and animators to pick up quickly.
- Highly readable: Python's clean code style makes it easy for teams to collaborate on large projects.
- Wide range of libraries: Python has libraries for almost everything, from machine learning to data analysis, 3D rendering, and even space exploration.
- Strong community: Python has a massive community of developers who constantly contribute new tools, libraries, and improvements, making it a continually evolving language.

Fun Fact: Python in Unexpected Places!
You might think Python is only for coding websites or scripts, but it is used in some unexpected places, too. Python plays a role in designing theme park rides, helping doctors analyze medical images, and even creating video games. Its versatility makes it useful in industries you wouldn't normally associate with programming!

Chapter 18: Python Projects - Fun Mini-Projects to Try

Project 1: Create a Virtual Pet (Where Users Take Care of a Digital Pet)

In this fun Python project, you'll create a **virtual pet**—a small, text-based game where users can interact with and care for a digital pet. The pet will have needs like **hunger, happiness**, and **energy**, and the player's goal is to keep the pet happy and healthy by feeding it, playing with it, and letting it rest.

This project is a great way to practice using **variables, loops, if statements**, and **functions** while building something interactive and fun!

Step 1: Defining the Pet's Needs

Our virtual pet will have three main needs:

1. **Hunger**: The pet will get hungry over time and needs to be fed.
2. **Happiness**: The pet will get sad if it doesn't get enough attention, so the player will need to play with it.
3. **Energy**: The pet will need to rest to keep its energy up.

Each of these needs will be represented by a **number** (like a score), which will change as the player interacts with the pet.

Code: Setting Up the Pet's Stats

```
class Pet:
    def __init__(self, name):
        self.name = name
        self.hunger = 50  # Hunger level (0 = full, 100 = starving)
        self.happiness = 50  # Happiness level (0 = sad, 100 = very happy)
        self.energy = 50  # Energy level (0 = tired, 100 = full of energy)

    def show_stats(self):
        print(f"{self.name}'s Stats: Hunger = {self.hunger}, Happiness = {self.happiness},
Energy = {self.energy}")
```

In this code:
- We create a **Pet** class that defines the pet's three main stats: **hunger, happiness,** and **energy.**
- The **show_stats()** method displays the pet's current stats to the player.

Step 2: Interacting with the Pet

Now we need to create functions that allow the player to interact with the pet. The player will be able to:
- **Feed** the pet to reduce hunger.
- **Play** with the pet to increase happiness.
- **Let the pet rest** to increase energy.

Code: Interacting with the Pet

```python
class Pet:
    def __init__(self, name):
        self.name = name
        self.hunger = 50
        self.happiness = 50
        self.energy = 50

    def show_stats(self):
        print(f"{self.name}'s Stats: Hunger = {self.hunger}, Happiness = {self.happiness}, Energy = {self.energy}")

    def feed(self):
        if self.hunger > 0:
            self.hunger -= 10
            print(f"You fed {self.name}. Hunger decreases!")
        else:
            print(f"{self.name} is full and doesn't need to eat!")

    def play(self):
        if self.energy > 10:
            self.happiness += 10
            self.energy -= 10
            print(f"You played with {self.name}. Happiness increases!")
        else:
            print(f"{self.name} is too tired to play.")
```

```
    def rest(self):
        if self.energy < 100:
            self.energy += 20
            print(f"{self.name} is resting. Energy increases!")
        else:
            print(f"{self.name} is already full of energy.")
```

In this section:

- The **feed()** function decreases the pet's hunger when the player feeds it.
- The **play()** function increases the pet's happiness and decreases energy when the player plays with it.
- The **rest()** function increases the pet's energy when it rests.

Step 3: Time-Based Needs

To make the game more challenging, the pet's stats will naturally decrease over time. The player will need to keep an eye on the pet's needs and interact with it before the hunger, happiness, or energy levels get too low. We'll create a function that **decays** the pet's stats as time passes, simulating the pet getting hungrier, sadder, or more tired.

Code: Time-Based Decay

```
import time

class Pet:
    def __init__(self, name):
        self.name = name
        self.hunger = 50
        self.happiness = 50
        self.energy = 50

    def show_stats(self):
        print(f"{self.name}'s Stats: Hunger = {self.hunger}, Happiness = {self.happiness},
Energy = {self.energy}")

    def feed(self):
        if self.hunger > 0:
            self.hunger -= 10
            print(f"You fed {self.name}. Hunger decreases!")
```

```python
        else:
            print(f"{self.name} is full and doesn't need to eat!")

    def play(self):
        if self.energy > 10:
            self.happiness += 10
            self.energy -= 10
            print(f"You played with {self.name}. Happiness increases!")
        else:
            print(f"{self.name} is too tired to play.")

    def rest(self):
        if self.energy < 100:
            self.energy += 20
            print(f"{self.name} is resting. Energy increases!")
        else:
            print(f"{self.name} is already full of energy.")

    def time_passes(self):
        self.hunger += 5
        self.happiness -= 5
        self.energy -= 5
        print(f"As time passes, {self.name}'s needs change.")
```

In this part:
- The **time_passes()** function simulates the passage of time by increasing **hunger** and decreasing **happiness** and **energy**.
- This function can be called repeatedly to simulate the pet's needs changing over time.

Step 4: Game Loop – Taking Care of the Pet

Now that we have all the basic functions in place, let's create a **game loop** where the player can continuously interact with the pet by choosing what to do (feed, play, rest) while the pet's stats decay over time.

Code: Game Loop

```python
def main():
    pet_name = input("What would you like to name your pet? ")
    pet = Pet(pet_name)
```

```python
    while True:
        pet.show_stats()
        action = input("What would you like to do? (feed/play/rest/quit): ").lower()

        if action == "feed":
            pet.feed()
        elif action == "play":
            pet.play()
        elif action == "rest":
            pet.rest()
        elif action == "quit":
            print(f"Goodbye, {pet_name}! Thanks for playing!")
            break
        else:
            print("Invalid option. Please choose feed, play, rest, or quit.")

        # Simulate time passing
        time.sleep(2)  # Wait 2 seconds
        pet.time_passes()

if __name__ == '__main__':
    main()
```

In this code:
- The **game loop** allows the player to continuously interact with the pet by choosing whether to **feed, play,** or let the pet **rest.**
- The **time_passes()** function is called after each action to simulate the pet's needs changing over time.
- The player can exit the game by typing **"quit".**

Fun Fact: Virtual Pets Were Hugely Popular in the 90s!
Before smartphones and apps, people played with virtual pets on small devices called Tamagotchis in the 90s. Players had to feed, play with, and take care of their Tamagotchi pets, just like in this game. These devices were a huge hit and laid the foundation for virtual pets in video games!

Project 2: Build a Simple Chatbot That Talks Back

In this project, we'll build a **simple chatbot** using Python. The chatbot can hold basic conversations, respond to questions, and tell jokes. While it won't be as advanced as AI-powered chatbots like Siri or Alexa, it is fun to practice using **if statements**, **variables**, and **loops**. You will also learn how to make the chatbot more interactive by giving it responses based on what the user says.

Step 1: Greeting the User

We will start by making the chatbot introduce itself and greet the user. This will make the chatbot feel more interactive right from the start.

Code: Chatbot Introduction

```
def greet_user():
    print("Hello! I'm ChatBot 3000. What's your name?")
    user_name = input("Enter your name: ")
    print(f"Nice to meet you, {user_name}! How can I help you today?")
    return user_name

# Call the function to start the conversation
greet_user()
```

In this part:
- The chatbot introduces itself and asks the user for their name.
- Once the user enters their name, the chatbot greets them personally using their name.

Step 2: Simple Responses Using If Statements

Next, we will teach the chatbot how to respond to some basic questions. We will use **if statements** to check the user's input and provide appropriate responses.

Code: Simple Chatbot Responses

```
def chatbot_response():
    print("You can ask me things like 'How are you?', 'Tell me a joke', or 'Goodbye'.")

    while True:
        user_input = input("You: ").lower()  # Convert the input to lowercase to handle case-insensitivity

        if "how are you" in user_input:
```

```
        print("ChatBot 3000: I'm just a bunch of code, but I'm doing great!")
    elif "joke" in user_input:
        print("ChatBot 3000: Why don't skeletons fight each other? Because they don't
have the guts!")
    elif "goodbye" in user_input:
        print("ChatBot 3000: Goodbye! Have a great day!")
        break  # Exit the chat loop
    else:
        print("ChatBot 3000: I'm not sure how to respond to that. Try asking something
else.")

# Call the function to start the chatbot conversation
chatbot_response()
```

In this section:
- The chatbot can now respond to a few simple prompts: "How are you?", "Tell me a joke", and "Goodbye".
- We use **if statements** to check the user's input and provide a response.
- If the user types "goodbye," the chatbot ends the conversation and exits the loop.

Step 3: Adding More Complex Responses

To make the chatbot more interactive, let's add responses that depend on **specific keywords** the user enters. This makes the chatbot feel more intelligent, as it can pick up on different topics and respond accordingly.

Code: Keyword-Based Responses

```
def chatbot_response():
    print("You can ask me anything or say 'goodbye' to end the chat.")

    while True:
        user_input = input("You: ").lower()

        if "weather" in user_input:
            print("ChatBot 3000: I don't have real weather data, but it looks like a great day
to learn Python!")
        elif "favorite" in user_input:
            print("ChatBot 3000: My favorite color is blue—because it's the color of the
internet!")
        elif "goodbye" in user_input:
```

221

```
            print("ChatBot 3000: Goodbye! I hope to chat with you again soon.")
            break
        else:
            print("ChatBot 3000: I didn't quite catch that. Could you ask something else?")
```

In this section:
- The chatbot now recognizes keywords like **"weather"** and **"favorite"** to provide relevant responses.
- If the chatbot doesn't understand the input, it prompts the user to ask another question.

Step 4: Random Responses for Variety

To make the chatbot feel more dynamic, we can add **random responses**. This way, the chatbot won't always say the same thing every time the user asks a certain question. We'll use Python's **random** module to choose a response from a list of possible answers.

Code: Adding Random Responses

```python
import random

def chatbot_response():
    jokes = [
        "Why don't skeletons fight each other? Because they don't have the guts!",
        "Why don't scientists trust atoms? Because they make up everything!",
        "What do you get when you cross a snowman with a vampire? Frostbite!"
    ]

    greetings = [
        "I'm doing great! Thanks for asking.",
        "Just code running smoothly, thanks for checking in!",
        "All systems are go! How about you?"
    ]

    print("You can ask me things like 'How are you?' or 'Tell me a joke', or say 'Goodbye'.")

    while True:
        user_input = input("You: ").lower()

        if "how are you" in user_input:
```

```
        print(f"ChatBot 3000: {random.choice(greetings)}")
    elif "joke" in user_input:
        print(f"ChatBot 3000: {random.choice(jokes)}")
    elif "goodbye" in user_input:
        print("ChatBot 3000: Goodbye! Have a great day!")
        break
    else:
        print("ChatBot 3000: I'm not sure how to respond to that. Try asking something
else.")
```

In this section:

- The chatbot has multiple **greetings** and **jokes**, and it picks one randomly each time the user asks about them.
- The **random.choice()** function is used to select a random response from a list, making the chatbot's answers feel more dynamic.

Step 5: Ending the Chat Politely

It's important for a chatbot to know when to end the conversation politely. The user can type **"goodbye"** at any time to finish the chat, and the chatbot will exit the loop.

Code: Ending the Conversation

```
def chatbot_response():
    print("You can chat with me or say 'goodbye' to end our conversation.")

    while True:
        user_input = input("You: ").lower()

        if "goodbye" in user_input:
            print("ChatBot 3000: Goodbye! Thanks for chatting!")
            break
        else:
            print("ChatBot 3000: Let's keep chatting! Ask me anything.")
```

In this section:
- If the user types "goodbye", the chatbot exits the loop and says a polite farewell.
- Otherwise, the conversation continues.

223

Project 3: Automate Something in Your Home

(Like Organizing Files or Setting Reminders)

Python is an excellent tool for automating small, everyday tasks in your
home, like **organizing files**, **setting reminders**, or even **renaming files
in bulk**. By writing simple Python scripts, you can save time on repetitive
tasks and make your computer do the work. In this project, we will walk
through two examples of home automation: **organizing files** and **setting
reminders**.

Step 1: Automating File Organization

We will start with a Python script that automatically organizes files in a
folder by their file type. For example, it will sort documents (like .txt and
.pdf files), images (like .jpg and .png files), and videos (like .mp4 and .avi
files) into separate folders.
This is especially useful if you frequently download or work with different
types of files and want to keep them organized.

Code: Organizing Files by Type

```python
import os
import shutil

def organize_files(folder_path):
    # Define the folder names for each file type
    file_types = {
        'Documents': ['.pdf', '.docx', '.txt'],
        'Images': ['.jpg', '.png', '.jpeg'],
        'Videos': ['.mp4', '.avi', '.mov'],
    }

    # Create the folders if they don't exist
    for folder in file_types.keys():
```

```
        os.makedirs(os.path.join(folder_path, folder), exist_ok=True)

    # Loop through all the files in the folder
    for filename in os.listdir(folder_path):
        file_path = os.path.join(folder_path, filename)

        # Skip directories
        if os.path.isdir(file_path):
            continue

        # Move files to the appropriate folder based on file extension
        file_extension = os.path.splitext(filename)[1]
        for folder, extensions in file_types.items():
            if file_extension in extensions:
                shutil.move(file_path, os.path.join(folder_path, folder, filename))
                break

# Provide the path to the folder you want to organize
folder_path = '/path/to/your/folder'
organize_files(folder_path)
```

How It Works:
- **os**: This module is used to interact with the file system, allowing you to create folders and move files.
- **shutil**: This module provides the ability to move files from one location to another.
- The script defines folders for each file type (e.g., Documents, Images, Videos) and automatically sorts files into these folders based on their file extensions.

How to Use It:
1. Replace the **/path/to/your/folder** with the actual path to the folder you want to organize.
2. Run the script, and it will automatically sort the files into their respective folders based on file type.

Step 2: Setting Automated Reminders

Next, let's automate reminders using Python. For example, you can create a script that sends you a reminder every day to water your plants, take a break, or check your emails. We will use the **time** and **schedule** libraries to schedule reminders at specific times.

Code: Setting Daily Reminders

```python
import schedule
import time

def send_reminder():
    print("Reminder: It's time to water your plants!")

# Schedule the reminder to run every day at 10:00 AM
schedule.every().day.at("10:00").do(send_reminder)

# Keep the script running
while True:
    schedule.run_pending()
    time.sleep(1)
```

How It Works:

- **schedule**: This library is used to schedule the reminder to run at specific times.
- **time.sleep(1)**: This keeps the program running continuously, checking for scheduled tasks every second.

How to Use It:

1. Customize the **message** in the **send_reminder()** function to fit whatever task you need to be reminded of (e.g., "Take a break!" or "Check your email!").
2. Adjust the time in **schedule.every().day.at("10:00")** to the time you want the reminder to go off.
3. Run the script, and it will automatically send you a reminder every day at the specified time.

Step 3: Customizing Your Reminders

You can easily customize this reminder system to fit your needs. For example, you could set up **multiple reminders** for different tasks throughout the day or make the reminder send you an email instead of printing to the console.

Example: Multiple Reminders

```
import schedule
import time

def water_plants_reminder():
    print("Reminder: It's time to water your plants!")

def take_break_reminder():
    print("Reminder: Take a 5-minute break!")

# Schedule multiple reminders
schedule.every().day.at("10:00").do(water_plants_reminder)
schedule.every().day.at("14:00").do(take_break_reminder)

# Keep the script running
while True:
    schedule.run_pending()
    time.sleep(1)
```

In this example:
- We have set up two reminders: one to water the plants at 10:00 AM and another to take a break at 2:00 PM.
- You can add as many reminders as you want by adding more **schedule.every()** lines for different tasks and times.

Step 4: Sending Email Reminders

If you want to take this a step further, you can send **email reminders** instead of just printing messages to the console. This is useful if you want to receive reminders on your phone or email app. We will use Python's **smtplib** library to send emails.

Code: Sending Email Reminders

```
import smtplib
from email.mime.text import MIMEText

def send_email_reminder():
    sender_email = "your_email@gmail.com"
    recipient_email = "recipient_email@example.com"
    subject = "Reminder: Water your plants!"
    body = "This is a friendly reminder to water your plants today."
```

```python
# Create the email content
message = MIMEText(body)
message['From'] = sender_email
message['To'] = recipient_email
message['Subject'] = subject

# Connect to the Gmail SMTP server and send the email
with smtplib.SMTP_SSL('smtp.gmail.com', 465) as server:
    server.login(sender_email, 'your_password')
    server.sendmail(sender_email, recipient_email, message.as_string())

# Schedule the email reminder for 10:00 AM every day
schedule.every().day.at("10:00").do(send_email_reminder)

# Keep the script running
while True:
    schedule.run_pending()
    time.sleep(1)
```

How It Works:
- **smtplib** is used to send an email through Gmail's SMTP server.
- **MIMEText** is used to format the email's subject and body.

How to Use It:
1. Replace **your_email@gmail.com** and **recipient_email@example.com** with the actual sender and recipient email addresses.
2. Replace **your_password** with your actual email password (note: for Gmail, you may need to generate an app-specific password).
3. Run the script, and it will send an email reminder every day at 10:00 AM.

Fun Fact: Automation Makes Life Easier!

Automation is all around us—think about how your phone can send you reminders to drink water, or how your smart home devices can turn off the lights at night. With Python, you can bring that same level of convenience to your own tasks, making your life a little easier!

Chapter 19: Where to Go Next?

Encouragement to Keep Learning and Exploring Python

Congratulations! You have come a long way in your Python journey, and now have a solid foundation to build on. From writing your first **"Hello, World!"** program to creating virtual pets, chatbots, and automating tasks, you have unlocked the door to endless possibilities with Python. But here is the exciting part—this is just the beginning!

Python is a vast and powerful language with so much more to explore. Whether you want to build complex web applications, dive into data science, or experiment with artificial intelligence, Python has the tools to help you achieve your goals. The key to mastering Python (or any skill) is to keep practicing, experimenting, and most importantly, having fun while you learn.

Why Keep Learning Python?

1. **It is Everywhere**: Python is used in virtually every field—whether it is web development, data science, game development, machine learning, or even space exploration. The skills you've learned so far can be applied to a wide variety of projects and career paths.
2. **It's Beginner-Friendly and Advanced**: Python is known for being easy to learn, but it is also powerful enough for experienced developers to tackle huge projects. This means that as you grow, Python will grow with you, supporting more complex ideas and challenges.
3. **You Can Build Anything**: With Python, you can create anything you dream of—from websites and games to AI models and data analysis tools. Python gives you the power to turn your ideas into reality, and you now have the skills to start creating!

Keep Experimenting

One of the best ways to keep learning is to **experiment** with your projects. Whether creating a simple app, automating tasks around your home, or building something entirely new, each project will teach you something valuable. Do not be afraid to break things, make mistakes, and learn from them—that is how real progress happens!

Here are a few ideas to spark your creativity:

- Build a personal website or blog using **Django** or **Flask**.
- Dive into **data science** with libraries like **Pandas** and **Matplotlib**.
- Create a simple **game** or **interactive story** with Python's **Pygame** library.
- Explore the world of AI and machine learning with Scikit-learn or TensorFlow.

The best part? You do not need to wait for someone to tell you what to do next. Python is a tool for building whatever you want. Let your imagination run wild!

Join the Python Community

You are not alone in your learning journey. Python has one of the world's largest and most supportive programming communities. Whether you are looking for help, inspiration, or feedback, a whole network of Python enthusiasts are eager to share their knowledge.

Here are some ways to stay connected:

- **Online forums** like Stack Overflow, Reddit's r/learnpython, or the Python Discord channel are great places to ask questions and find tutorials.
- **GitHub** is a platform where developers share their projects. You can contribute to open-source projects or even share your work.
- **Python meetups** and conferences happen worldwide. Look for virtual events or local meetups where you can learn from others and even showcase your projects.

> Fun Fact: Python's Creator Loves Monty Python!
> Did you know that the name "Python" comes from the British comedy group Monty Python? Python's creator, Guido van Rossum, was a big fan of their work, and he chose the name as a nod to the group's playful and creative spirit. That same playfulness can be found in Python's simplicity and versatility. So as you continue learning, remember to keep a sense of fun and creativity—just like Python was designed to inspire!

Links to Online Resources and Communities

As you continue your Python journey, plenty of excellent online resources and communities help you learn, find inspiration, and troubleshoot problems. Whether you are looking for tutorials, courses, coding challenges, or a place to connect with other Python enthusiasts, these resources have covered you. Here is a list of some of the best websites and communities to explore:

Python.org

Website: Python.org

Why It's Great: Python's official website is a treasure trove of documentation, tutorials, and resources for all levels of learners. You can download the latest version of Python, access detailed documentation, and find links to events and Python-related news.

What You will Find:

- Official Python documentation.
- A list of Python tutorials.
- Links to Python **conferences** and **meetups**.

GitHub

Website: GitHub

Why It's Great: GitHub is a platform for hosting and sharing code. You can explore thousands of Python projects, contribute to open-source projects, or host your own code for others to see.

What You will Find:

- **Open-source Python projects** that you can contribute to.
- A place to **share your own code** and get feedback from others.
- The ability to **collaborate** with developers around the world on coding projects.

Fun Fact: Python Has One of the Largest Developer Communities!
Python's popularity has exploded over the past decade, and with millions of developers around the world, you'll never be short of people to learn from and collaborate with. No matter where you are in your Python journey, the Python community is there to support you!

Encouragement to Keep Learning and Exploring Python

As you reach the end of this book, it is important to remember that this is just the beginning of your Python journey. You have taken the first steps in learning a powerful and versatile programming language that opens up endless possibilities. But there is always more to discover, more projects to build, and more problems to solve. Python is a tool that grows with you—whether you are a beginner writing your first "Hello, World!" program or an experienced developer tackling complex projects.

Keep Practicing and Experimenting

The key to mastering Python, or any skill, is practice. The more you experiment, the better you will get at solving problems and building things on your own. Do not be afraid to try new projects or tackle challenges that seem difficult. With Python, you can:

- **Build games** and applications.
- **Automate tasks** to make life easier.
- Explore data science and machine learning.
- Create websites and web apps.
- Contribute to open-source projects.

Python is like a toolkit that you can use to build just about anything. So, keep challenging yourself with new projects and ideas. Every mistake you make is just a step toward learning something new!

Do not Be Afraid to Make Mistakes

Programming can be tricky, and mistakes are part of the learning process. Every great programmer has faced challenges, bugs, and errors. The important thing is to keep trying and learn from those mistakes. Python is a forgiving language that encourages exploration and experimentation. So, if something does not work the way you expect it to, that is okay! Debugging and problem-solving are valuable skills that will make you a better coder.

Explore New Areas of Python

Now that you've learned the basics, it is time to start exploring new areas of Python. There are so many paths you can take, and each one offers something exciting and different. Here are a few ideas to help guide your next steps:

- **Web Development**: Learn how to create websites and web applications using **Django** or **Flask**.
- **Data Science and Machine Learning**: Dive into **Pandas**, **Numpy**, and **Matplotlib** to analyze data, or explore machine learning with **Scikit-learn** and **TensorFlow**.

- **Automation**: Automate repetitive tasks like file organization, sending emails, or scraping websites.
- **Game Development**: Create your own games using Python's **Pygame** library.
- **Artificial Intelligence**: Explore the world of AI by learning how to train models and build intelligent applications.

Each area offers new challenges and opportunities to grow as a developer.

Stay Curious and Keep Exploring

The most important thing in your learning journey is to stay curious. Python is constantly evolving, and new tools, libraries, and frameworks are always being developed. Be open to trying new things, and never stop asking questions. Whether it is figuring out how to solve a problem, learning a new library, or contributing to an open-source project, there is always something exciting waiting for you to explore.

Join the Python Community

Python has one of the largest and most supportive communities in the world. If you ever get stuck, need inspiration, or want to collaborate on a project, the Python community is here to help. Whether you join online forums, contribute to open-source projects, or attend Python meetups, connecting with other Python learners and developers will give you fresh ideas and valuable support.

Fun Fact: Python Is in Space!
Did you know that Python is used in NASA's projects, including space exploration? Python plays a big role in helping scientists analyze data from space missions and create simulations of spacecraft behavior. Python truly has no limits, and your Python journey could take you anywhere—even beyond the stars!

Fun Fact: The World of Coding Is Always Growing, and You Can Be Part of It!

The world of coding is constantly evolving, and Python is right at the heart of this growth. Every day, developers are creating new tools, building innovative apps, and solving global problems with code. From smartphones to social media, online shopping to space exploration—coding is shaping the future, and you have the chance to be part of it!

Here are a few cool facts about how coding is shaping our world:

Coding Powers Almost Everything

Did you know that the code you have learned in Python can be found in almost everything we use daily? From the apps on your phone to the websites you visit and the software that powers your favorite games—coding makes it all possible. And it is not just limited to software—**smart home devices**, **robotics**, and even **cars** use code to operate. The possibilities are endless!

Python Is Helping Fight Global Challenges

Python is being used in **scientific research**, **medicine**, and **climate science** to solve some of the world's biggest challenges. Whether it's helping doctors analyze medical images, predicting climate change patterns, or designing robots that can assist with surgery, Python is making a huge impact. With the knowledge you've gained, you could contribute to solving these real-world problems too!

New Technologies Are Always Emerging

The tech world is full of new and exciting developments. From **artificial intelligence (AI)** and **machine learning** to **blockchain** and **virtual reality (VR)**, coding is at the forefront of creating technologies that will change how we live. By continuing to learn and code, you'll be at the cutting edge of these innovations.

Anyone Can Be a Coder

The best part about coding is that **anyone can learn it**—no matter where you're from or what you do. Coders come from all walks of life; there is always room for more. You do not need to be a math genius or have a fancy degree to start coding. All it takes is curiosity, a willingness to learn, and a bit of practice. You are already well on your way!

The Python Community Is Here to Help

Coding is not just about writing lines of code—it is about being part of a global community of creators, problem-solvers, and innovators. The Python community is one of the largest and most welcoming programming communities. Whether contributing to **open-source projects,** collaborating on new ideas, or helping someone else learn, you are part of something much bigger. And the best part? You do not have to do it alone!

Why You Should Stay Excited About Coding

The world of technology is growing so quickly that the things we consider futuristic today could become everyday realities tomorrow. Just look at how fast **self-driving cars, smart assistants,** and **robotics** are evolving. As a Python programmer, you are stepping into a world where **your skills can shape the future.** Who knows? The next big idea could come from you!

Fun Fact: There Are Over 23 Million Developers Worldwide!
That's right—coding is a global skill, with millions of developers working on incredible projects daily. As more people join the coding community, the innovation potential grows. You're now part of this ever-expanding world, and the skills you've learned in Python are just the beginning
.

Glossary

This glossary contains definitions for all the important Python concepts, terms, and structures covered throughout the book. Use it as a quick reference to reinforce your understanding as you continue learning and building Python projects.

Algorithm

- Definition: A sequence of steps or instructions that the computer follows to solve a problem.
- Example: Sorting a list of numbers from smallest to largest.

Argument

- Definition: The value or data you pass to a function when calling it.
- Example: In print("Hello"), the argument is "Hello".

Assignment

- Definition: Storing a value in a variable using the = symbol.
- Example: age = 25 assigns the value 25 to the variable age.

Binary

- Definition: The base-2 number system that computers use to represent data, using only 0s and 1s.
- Example: The number 2 in binary is represented as 10.

Boolean

- Definition: A data type with two possible values: True or False.
- Example: is_raining = True is a Boolean variable storing the value True.

Built-in Function

- Definition: Functions that come with Python, like print(), len(), and input().
- Example: print("Hello, World!") is using the built-in print() function.

Class

- Definition: A blueprint for creating objects. A class defines attributes (properties) and methods (functions) that the objects will have.
- Example:

```
class Dog:
  def __init__(self, name):
    self.name = name
```

Comment

- Definition: A note in the code that is not executed. Used to explain code and make it easier to understand. In Python, comments start with #.
- Example: # This is a comment.

Compiler

Definition: A program that converts the entire code into machine language before running it. Python is an interpreted language, but other languages like C use compilers.
Example: In Python, the interpreter reads and executes code line by line.

Conditional (If Statement)

- Definition: A statement that checks a condition and executes code based on whether the condition is True or False.
- Example:

```
if age >= 18:
            print("You are an adult.")
```

Data Type

- Definition: A category of data that defines what kind of value a variable can hold (e.g., integers, floats, strings, Booleans).
- Example: 42 is an integer, 3.14 is a float, and "Hello" is a string.

Dictionary

- Definition: A data type that stores data in key-value pairs, where each key is associated with a value.
- Example

```
student = {"name": "Alice", "age": 25, "grade": "A"}
```

Exception

- Definition: An error that occurs during the execution of a program. Python handles exceptions using try and except blocks to prevent the program from crashing.
- Example

```
try:
    number = int(input("Enter a number: "))
except ValueError:
    print("Invalid input!")
```

Float

- Definition: A data type that represents decimal numbers.
- Example: 3.14 and 9.99 are float values.

For Loop

- Definition: A loop that iterates over a sequence (like a list, tuple, or string) and executes a block of code for each item in the sequence.
- Example:

```
for fruit in ["apple", "banana", "cherry"]:
    print(fruit)
```

Function

- Definition: A reusable block of code that performs a specific task. You can define your own functions or use built-in ones.
- Example:

```
def greet(name):
    print(f"Hello, {name}")
```

If Statement

- Definition: A control structure that executes a block of code only if a specified condition is True.
- Example:

```
if temperature > 30:
    print("It's hot!")
```

Import
- Definition: The process of loading a module or library into your program so you can use its functions and variables.
- Example:

```
import random
```

Indentation

- Definition: The spaces or tabs used at the beginning of lines of code to define blocks in Python, such as loops, conditionals, and functions.
- Example:

```
if True:
    print("This line is indented")
```

Input

- Definition: A built-in function that allows the user to enter data from the keyboard.
- Example:

```
name = input("Enter your name: ")
```

Integer

- Definition: A data type that represents whole numbers, both positive and negative.
- Example: 5, 0, and 12 are all integers.

Interpreter

- Definition: A program that reads and executes code line by line. Python is an interpreted language.
- Example: When you run a Python script, the interpreter reads and executes it one line at a time.

List

- Definition: A collection of items that are ordered and changeable. Lists are one of Python's most versatile data types.

241

- Example:

```
fruits = ["apple", "banana", "cherry"]
```

Loop

- Definition: A structure that repeats a block of code multiple times. The two main types of loops in Python are for loops and while loops.
- Example:

```
while count < 10:
    print(count)
    count += 1
```

Method

- Definition: A function that is associated with an object and can modify the object's state or perform actions with it.
- Example:

```
my_list = [1, 2, 3]
my_list.append(4)  # append is a method that adds an item to
the list
```

Module

- Definition: A file that contains Python code, such as functions and variables, that you can import and use in other scripts.
- Example:

```
import math
print(math.sqrt(25))
```

Return

- Definition: A statement used in functions to send a value back to the caller.
- Example:

```
def add(a, b):
    return a + b
```

String

- Definition: A sequence of characters used to represent text. Strings are enclosed in quotation marks.
- Example: "Hello, World!" is a string.

Syntax

- Definition: The set of rules that defines how Python code is written and structured.
- Example: Python uses indentation to define blocks of code, unlike many other languages that use braces {}.

Tuple

- Definition: A collection of items that are ordered and unchangeable (immutable). Tuples are similar to lists but cannot be modified after creation.
- Example:

```
colors = ("red", "green", "blue")
```

Variable

- Definition: A name that stores data in a program. Variables can store different types of data like numbers, strings, or Booleans.

- Example:

```
name = "Alice"
age = 25
```

While Loop

- Definition: A loop that repeats a block of code as long as a specific condition is True.
- Example:

```
while count < 5:
    print(count)
    count += 1
```

Fun Fact: Python's Simplicity
Python's straightforward syntax and readability make it a popular choice for beginners and experienced developers alike. Its wide range of applications, from web development to artificial intelligence, ensures that Python will continue to be a leading language for years to come.

www.ingramcontent.com/pod-product-compliance
Lightning Source LLC
LaVergne TN
LVHW051223050326
832903LV00028B/2241